Endorsemen

All we ever ask of our EOS® clients is that they are open and honest with each other. If everyone were, it would change the world or, at a minimum, their company. This book is the how-to manual for being open and honest. I highly recommend it.

—Gino Wickman
Author of *Traction* and *Shine*, Creator of EOS®

What Ken and Grace have created is transforming lives from the bedroom to the boardroom and everywhere in between. This is more than just a book. It's an authentic, heart-felt story. A mirror. A tool. It's an inspirational and crystal-clear path to a better you and a better us, making for a better world.

—Lisa Cooper
Founder and Chief People Officer
Cooper People Group

Know Honesty beautifully breaks down two core tenets toward transformational trust building: human connection and healthy communication: truly being open and honest. The 6 practices outlined create a simple roadmap for becoming our best and making a meaningful, authentic impact in our ever-evolving world.

—Kelly Knight
President and Integrator, EOS Worldwide

Communication is the key to success, whether it's with your loved ones or those you work alongside, we are simply better humans when we are open and honest. Ken and Grace have developed a simple proven process to develop open and honest relationships. Our team has agreed to meet others where they are, lean in, listen to understand, and accept the thoughts of others. In doing so, our relationships are stronger, our attention to the vision is laser focused, and our success has been unbelievably astronomical. All great things take work, but using the Know Honesty pathway has provided us with a north star in terms of communication.

—Bev Thiel
Executive Director, Habitat for Humanity® Kent County, Michigan

Ken and Grace have created practical, compelling, and understandable tools for anyone with the desire to improve their communication with others.

—Rick Baker
President and CEO, Grand Rapids Chamber of Commerce

If you are looking to reduce your anxiety about interactions and conversations you have with other people, the practices Ken and Grace share in this book will be a powerful tool for you. Since implementing The Agreement in a few of my closest relationships, I have felt free to be myself without restriction. It's the strongest unlock I've had in my thirties.

—Jeff Pipp
CEO, Bloom Social

KNOW HONESTY

ELIMINATE THE DIVIDE, BECOME A MASTERFUL COMMUNICATOR, AND CONNECT WITH ANYONE

KNOW HONESTY

ELIMINATE THE DIVIDE, BECOME A MASTERFUL COMMUNICATOR, AND CONNECT WITH ANYONE

KEN BOGARD AND GRACE GAVIN

ethos
collective

Published by Ethos Collective™
P.O. Box 43, Powell, OH 43065
EthosCollective.vip

LCCN: 2024914882
Paperback ISBN: 978-1-63680-344-9
Hardcover ISBN: 978-1-63680-345-6
e-book ISBN: 978-1-63680-346-3

Available in paperback, hardcover, e-book, and audiobook.

Dedication

Ken
For all the humans trying to navigate this crazy life together.

Grace
*For Dad, thank you for showing me the value of hard work,
continuous learning, and fully living each day.*

Table of Contents

Part III: Openness and Honesty in Action

Preface

Why This Work Matters

By picking up this book, you've acknowledged the glaring communication issues we have today. We are more disconnected than ever and suffering the consequences. It is killing our relationships, our businesses, and our society.

But this doesn't have to be how we live. We have the choice, every day, to choose connection over isolation. Our communication can become a gift again and eliminate the divide between ourselves and others. You can learn to be a masterful communicator and connect with anyone.

We have spent years understanding, pushing, testing, and modeling an approach that gives people greater levels of identity and freedom. Through our work and research, we've helped countless individuals develop the necessary skills to do better together and get what they really want out of life. Be prepared, as applying what follows in this book will transform you and your relationships.

We'll share real stories from our lives and our clients, many of which you've experienced in your own life. Alongside our stories, you'll be equipped with the education and The

Six Practices™ we've developed. And because we know the world is moving faster, we've designed it to be put into action immediately.

While writing this book and doing this work, many people have asked us, "Why? What is the mission we've decided to dedicate so much of our time and resources toward? Where does the empathy and relentless commitment to helping others come from?" In the following stories, we'll share our why, but the overall answer is simple: *We're here to change how the world communicates.*

From Ken

I've found these to be the toughest questions to answer because the responses require such a high level of honesty and letting people in. Like most, I am not always comfortable doing so. But that is precisely why this book matters. I cannot ask others to do what I am first unwilling to do myself, and so below is my answer to why.

My dad raised me as a single father from when I was two years old. I would best describe him as a stoic German, Lutheran, retired engineer, and former military. Suffice it to say he was a man of few words. I distinctly remember my father saying, "I am not your friend; I am your father." That is the nature of my beginnings.

Because he was a man of few words and unwilling to discuss emotions deeper than the surface level, the word *bullying* didn't appear in our vocabulary. You deal with the cards you're dealt. I hadn't heard of bullying as it is understood today and, therefore, didn't have any idea of what it was. But that didn't stop me from experiencing it.

By the time I was eight, I was riding my bike to school by myself. Every day, I would pass by a group of kids waiting for the bus. One day, I heard a *plink!* I shrugged it off. The next day, *plink! plink!* I realized stones were being chucked my way. I figured some kids thought they were funny and kept on moving. But the next day, it was over the top. They tossed several stones and laughed as I rode by. As a kid, I couldn't understand why. What did I do to deserve this? I was simply on my way to school, just like them.

I hid this experience from my father. I'd gotten the clear message by then that I had to deal with the problem. So I biked on, doing my best to avoid a stone to the head and pedaling as fast as I could when passing them. I ducked and dodged their throws until one day when a stone got stuck in my front wheel. I went flying over the handlebars, skinning my hands and body as I collided with the pavement. I turned toward them and screamed the worst phrase I could muster at eight years old, "GO TO HELL!"

That hatred I spewed at them did nothing to stop them from picking up the stones again the next day. This behavior continued for weeks until someone finally noticed it and put an end to my pain and suffering. To this day, I don't know whether it was a parent, another kid, or a school authority who stepped up. I had never mentioned it to anyone. After all, I'd learned not to talk about it, just deal with it.

These instances of bullying followed me throughout my childhood. I was again on my bike at ten years old, heading home this time, when a group of teenagers driving by in their car started yelling at me. Their tone felt threatening, and fear coursed through me. I watched as they turned around and drove back toward me. I zipped into our condominium complex, hoping that would stop them, but they continued their chase. Having no other choice, I slid my bike under some pine trees and skidded down an embankment, hoping they wouldn't find me. I found myself in yet another situation I couldn't understand. What did I do to deserve being chased and terrified?

Around the same age, some adults threatened me and my friend by flashing a gun at us. Why? A boy chucked a football at my head while I was playing by myself on a merry-go-round. My head snapped and bounced off the sharp metal frame, splitting the skin above my eye. Blood poured over my face, and I needed several stitches. Why? Later in life, while attending a boarding school for my freshman and sophomore years, kids would "penny in" our dorm room doors, locking my roommate and me inside. Why? There were other instances, such as kids who poured water under our doors to ruin our clothes and homework. We were pelted with objects and often wrestled to the ground. Why? These instances became commonplace for me. But I never considered it bullying; I just kept quiet and played the cards I had been dealt.

I'm aware of the millions of childhoods that were filled with suffering far greater than mine. Regardless, each one of these occurrences left me questioning this cruel human treatment of each other. At the time, the question remained unanswered due to the lack of communication in our home.

Looking back, I understand now the profound effect it had on me—it absolutely destroyed my self-worth. As a child without the tools to understand these experiences, I was left to my own conclusions. I reasoned that these cruelties must have happened because I was less than and didn't matter nearly as much as anyone else in my life. My opinions and thoughts weren't worthy of expression.

And yet amidst all this, I remained the kid who was able to listen to others, care for them, and protect them from what I experienced. I was the kid who would listen but didn't have the self-worth to express who I was, what I wanted, or how I was of value to anyone's life. That all changed as I hit my teenage years. All those moments of bullying, feeling threatened, taking nicks to my soul, and being antagonized had accumulated and created a monster.

By seventeen, I grew into semi-decent smarts and semi-decent looks—and built a stronger physique on top of that. My ego skyrocketed, and long gone was the little boy capable of listening and concerning himself with others. Those pent-up moments where people took advantage of my fear morphed me into a self-serving beast. I completely ostracized my father by creating thick and impenetrable walls between us. I ruined my relationship with the one person who really gave it his all for his son. No one else mattered more than me. That same treatment spilled into so many more lives around me.

As the years progressed, I chose professions that served me and had little outward positive impact. I selected relationships that appeased only me. After seventeen years of faith and religion, I turned my back on my Maker and His teachings, slowly separating myself from a moral compass. I used brutal honesty as a weapon against anyone close to me. To anyone who challenged me, I made witty comebacks that trounced them. I learned to turn on the charm whenever it would benefit me. Real relationships were not a thing; instead, I idolized the icons who were just as self-absorbed and money-hungry as I was. I was creating and maintaining myself as one of the worst types of human beings to be around. I had become everything I used to hate. In search of self-worth, I sprinted down a path that almost guaranteed I'd never truly experience it.

By the time I hit my mid-twenties, I was the emptiest I had ever felt. On the outside, it seemed that I had immense confidence, but I knew internally I had become a shell of a person. Not a single relationship in my life could be considered wholly genuine. There was substance abuse, dead-end jobs, and empty romantic relationships going nowhere. Everything existed simply as a means of pacifying myself. At some moments, I didn't care anymore about anything. It all felt as if both the world and I had darkened by the day. That emptiness and isolation nearly took my life.

I didn't know what to do or who to talk to about any of this. After all, I had pushed away every person who so much as attempted to get close. And then I remembered the one thing my father always stressed: prayer. But even prayer required opening up to Someone or Something. Having no other solution, I stood in the bathroom of a friend's rented basement apartment and fell to my knees. I let out all the emotions I'd closed myself off from and finally humbled myself. I prayed and prayed for help to Someone I had completely rejected. At that moment, I decided to let God in, even as I wasn't sure I believed, through the brick wall I had built. That one small moment of openness brought all the walls crumbling down, and my eyes were opened.

I saw how my false sense of self-protection left me stranded, with only those suffocating walls surrounding me. No wonder things felt lonely and purposeless. That day on the bathroom floor, I finally saw how all my self-serving and egotistical ways could only lead to me being alone. The whole time, I was trying to design a world for one when the world was designed for many.

And that is why I'm committed to helping others. I've seen what happens to our relationships and our world when all people do is serve themselves first. When we develop a "me, myself, and I" approach, we foster a deep disregard for everyone else in the world. Rather than connecting and caring for others, we erect endless divides. The results will never satisfy us when they are bred in a vat of selfishness. And in the end, they prevent us from getting what we really want and need for ourselves and for those around us.

In my life, I have watched families ripped apart, companies destroyed, and friendships lost because of an inability to be open and honest. We are quickly creating larger rips in the fabric of our society and damaging any hope we have of doing better together. And so, Grace and I have decided to do something about it—to not sit idly by as our culture devolves into its worst inhibitions.

From Grace

I've often been asked some form of the following question: "Why are you doing this work?" Which is really a question of "Why does it matter to me?" I share so many stories and reasons with people who ask this question. In working with teams and individuals, I watch remarkable transformations take place as people create genuine communication and real relationships. It is the most beautiful and privileged experience, and I get to be a part of it.

But as I sat alone with the question, prodding deeper and asking for 100 percent honesty of myself, I kept coming back to an experience that has touched every aspect of my life and will do so for all that is yet to come. It lives between my work and personal life, informs the decisions I make, and is my greatest failure of honesty. And to tell this story, I must give you some background.

I was born the daughter of dairy farmers in a small town, within a devout faith tradition, and the last of eight strong and opinionated children. My father, John, was the dreamer and doer. He pushed himself, his wife, and his children every day to work hard. "We got a lotta work to do today," was his chosen phrase. Growing up, I didn't understand why it seemed that he missed so much of my childhood in favor of the farm and work. I simply couldn't understand that that was his way of providing for us, in the only way he knew how. Sharing his emotions and vulnerabilities was not in his wheelhouse, like most men of his generation.

And then came July 14, 2020. During a global pandemic, when I thought life couldn't possibly get any more complicated, Dad went to the ER with pains and was admitted for testing. At sixty-seven years old, he wasn't the picture of health, but to me, he looked like every older farmer I knew. I never thought I would see my father lying in a hospital bed, unsure of what the results might be and doing his best to stay positive.

After days and several tests, we had our answer: small cell carcinoma, stage four. A stubborn fighter through and through, Dad started chemo in the hospital and was released after twelve days. Our family rallied around him, made support plans, and celebrated his birthday a week later. He took his medications, went to chemotherapy, and tried his best to stay involved in the farm.

But what no one in the family, myself included, would talk about was the survival rate for the advanced stage and type of cancer he had. My father had a less than 3 percent chance of survival. We spent months avoiding the topic, losing out on precious time. It was passed around in small, hushed whispers between individuals, but not one of us was brave enough to be honest about what we were facing.

For me, there was only one such conversation with my sister Rose in an upstairs bedroom of our parents' house. She had done her research and shared the survival statistics with me, wondering aloud if what we were doing, clinging to the hope of an impossible miracle, was truly the best use of the limited time we had left with him. I knew in my heart she was right, but I couldn't allow myself to truly hear her—to absorb the words she shared and make a change while we still had time. I left that conversation shaken, wishing I could erase it from my mind. I said nothing, no one else uttered the truth for all to hear, and our journey of fighting a losing battle continued. And five short months later, on December 28, 2020, Dad left this earth.

There is no do-over for our greatest failing to say what needed to be said. Because of that, we lost all the time we had left hiding from it rather than facing it head-on. So many of my dad's stories went unheard because I turned away from what we knew was coming and pretended I'd have forever to hear the stories and spend more time with him.

And while people have told me that we never could have known what would happen, we did know the odds and the risks associated with all the treatments. We watched as this once giant of a man, opinionated and stubborn, seemingly melted away before our eyes. And yet we could not be honest about it.

This is why I push so hard for this work. Because I know what happens when we don't embrace the circumstances life has given us with an open heart and an honest mind. We lose out on all the connections and relationships offered to us. I ran from it and lost so much because of that. It is a regret I carry with me all my days. Don't let it be a regret you carry too. Today, I sit in a position that is well-informed. I understand the fragility of these moments. I take more time to embrace people for who they are and what they stand for. I recognize that we have only one life to live in a way I never used to.

I am sharing this experience with you and for you.

From Ken and Grace

We're here to be a force for good, to help foster connection, and, ultimately, change how the world communicates.

In doing so, we've written this book for the change-makers, whether you're reading as a growth-oriented individual or an organizational leader ready to revolutionize your people and your culture. What follows is education, practices rooted in reality, and stories of authentic transformation.

Let's begin Your Pursuit.

PART I

Real Communication = Open + Honest Communication

1

No Two People:
Why Communication Fails

What if we told you that just two words could set you free? And that in understanding what they mean and living them out each day, you could magnify what it means to be alive and live a happier, more fulfilled life? Your daily interactions would become more fluid, and the stressors of each day would be, well, less stressful. In these two words you'll find the key to unlocking what it is you really want. You'll find a new level of freedom for yourself and those around you.

Before now, you've heard these words but might not have paused to consider the power held within them. Those two words are: *open* and *honest*.

Picture the flow of water in your mind. Imagine for a moment that rain clouds contain some of the purest water. These clouds are resting just above a mountain, and it begins pouring rain. This pure, refreshing beginning is the kind of water we all wish was available in abundance. But as it hits the mountainside, immediately that purity erodes. As it flows forth, it picks up dirt, moss, and whatever else might be on the mountainside until it becomes undrinkable, even to the point of sickness. The flow turns and bends as it encounters rocks and fallen trees, guaranteeing its path is never the most efficient it could be. When the water finally joins the other streams running down to create a collective river, it becomes a powerful force, one that is paradoxically life-giving or life-destroying.

Our communication as human beings is quite similar. When we engage in conversation, we have the choice to give the gift of pure communication, or we can pollute it by adding in unnecessary and, often, damaging lies, half-truths, and façades. In return, we can choose to receive someone else's communication fully and in its purest form or we put up the equivalent of rocks and trees to block our own ability to receive it. As we try to communicate, much like the water flowing down the mountainside, our communication becomes distorted, polluted, and, ultimately, life-destroying.

Day in and day out, we observe that people abuse and misuse communication, slowing their ability to adapt, grow, and learn, ultimately making the communication a detriment. The barriers they put between themselves stop the free flow of information. One person's words erupt toward another, thrashing the water aggressively, splashing all over the place, and losing the intended effect. Another blocks the water from even reaching them, as if to say, "Your water is not good enough." Some tainted their water with other guises and lies, ruining the original contents.

This lack of clarity and purity, like the water by the time it reaches the river, is making us sick. It slows down our ability to communicate, discuss issues effectively, and find a solution. Our tainted communication is stopping us from experiencing real relationships and inhibiting us from getting what we want. Communication is our connective life force. It is how we use and exchange information. It's our main source for growth. And when you understand the importance of communication, you ought to want it in its purest form.

That form takes shape when communication is both open and honest. If you take anything away from this book, let it be the very next two lines.

By open, we mean listening without reservation, putting your needs and wants on pause for someone else.

By honest, we mean being truly and freely yourself, speaking into what you want and how you feel.

When we're able to exchange communication that is open and honest, we're operating at the purest level possible, removing any filters or blocks that inhibit our ability to connect. That is when we're creating *real communication*, exchanging as 100 percent open and 100 percent honest. That's what we're after in every single conversation—communication where everyone is heard and respected.

Reversing the Mess We've Made

The cultures we're creating and inheriting today struggle deeply to communicate. And the reason why is simple: those at the helm refuse to embrace being open and honest. This refusal breaks down our ability to do better together. A quick scan gives us a multitude of scenarios where this is happening:

Most organizations, their leadership, and their employees struggle to create and exist in environments where the communication flows freely between one another. Instead, we choose to value other metrics first. We quickly forget the importance of human connection and blind our eyes with the end objective, forgoing the how and togetherness. We then act surprised when our turnover rate is high, and engagement is low.

Geographically, we see it when two nations at odds won't communicate, let alone work toward real communication with openness and honesty. They embrace stubborn ideologies, unwilling to allow any other to exist but their own—which often leads to war and the unnecessary deaths of those on both sides. The need for control runs deep within the leadership of such nations and ultimately only serves themselves.

Well-intended marriages and relationships suffer because of the desperate lack of communication, making it ever more difficult to navigate the simplest of conversations. Recently, Ken joked to someone, "How is it that the entire world is not divorced?" The reply was, "It is." Nearly 50 percent of first marriages end in divorce, and second marriages are closer to 60 percent. Our lack of commitment to one another is through the roof. Humans turn away from each other rather than toward each other; we choose the lazier path of disconnectedness over commitment to one another's collective problems.

Social media platforms are hardly social in any positive or concrete means. We can drop in and out quickly, leave a scathing comment, and simply walk away unwilling to engage in any form of productive conversation. The screens have served as a giant blockade, allowing us to ignore the living and breathing person on the other side of our posts and comments. Social media is a place to point our proverbial guns at one another and retreat to cover without a scratch, leaving others wounded in our selfish wakes.

We continue to create environments that suffocate any opportunity for real communication. Instead, we elect for what will serve us best, whether that means escaping a difficult conversation, holding tightly to our worldview, or taking up all the attention within a space for just ourselves.

We are in desperate need of people at the helm willing to stand, promote, and drive home openness and honesty. That is how we will experience real freedom, for ourselves and for everyone else. Peace comes with knowing we all have a space for our honesty because everyone else in our lives is willing to be open, and they will have their opportunity to be truly and freely themselves too.

This is the battle. This is the collective problem we face. It's now time to reverse our mess. We can rectify the environments and cultures and no longer remain stuck. We have a choice. It's time to help teams, organizations, and individuals be more open and honest and change the tide.

A Universal Truth to Move Us Forward

Every moment of disagreement is an opportunity to reverse our historical abuse of communication. Working with clients, we've discovered a universal truth: No two people on this planet will walk through life together, agreeing completely. Think about it for a moment. No two out of eight billion people in this world can pair up and agree on every single topic. We won't ever completely align with one another. In fact, people rarely see things the same way. We constantly encounter and create conflicts and disagreements. And that is okay. In fact, it is normal and perfectly acceptable. Disagreement is as prevalent as oxygen. But we've come to avoid, reject, and even hate those with whom we disagree.

The reality is that we've all entered into this world designed for many yet treat it as though it were designed for one. That hardly leaves room for anyone else. We've put on blinders. We've prioritized ourselves. We intentionally and unintentionally trampled over others to serve ourselves first. We're actively creating distance and disruption between one another because the discomfort of being in conflict has become too intolerable. From mundane differences to deeper, more opposing controversial topics, we've come to believe that our point of view is the only correct one. And in doing so, we inadvertently form a chasm between one another. By refusing to accept that others see the world differently than we do, we make it harder and harder to navigate this shared world. What we must recognize is that our coexistence within a shared and interconnected world largely depends on one item: communication.

Ken shares the following:

I will never forget sitting in one of my first college marketing classes. Professor Robert Frey, an international executive of the Whirlpool Corporation, taught the class. I was thrilled to be in the presence of a professor with real-world experience as deep and rich as his. On the first day of class, he shared an important concept with us that would change the course of my life.

Addressing the classroom, he said, "The single biggest issue with companies is…"

I remember getting ready to write this profound, groundbreaking statement. I was thrilled that I was about to get my money's worth for this college education.

Then, he delivered the answer: "communication."

I dropped my pen, thinking, "What a joke!" I couldn't believe that communication was the single biggest issue companies deal with. What about strategy? What about talent? As a nineteen-year-old, I thought, "There is no way that grown human beings can't communicate." I didn't buy it and totally discounted his statement. But here's the deal—he was 100 percent correct.

As souls navigating this life, we can articulate our wants and needs better than any other species on the planet. Yet, we don't do it. We rarely communicate as purely as we can. We're often unclear about how we truly feel or what we really want. We taint our communication, deepening the chasm between us and reducing the understanding we could have of one another. We've positioned ourselves in a false sense of reality. The depth of our communication is an amazing gift. It allows us to accomplish remarkable things together, like putting a man on the moon, building skyscrapers thousands of feet high, or finding cures for horrible diseases. But that doesn't mean we take full advantage of this gift. In fact, it seems we are squandering it faster than ever. We can't communicate. Not effectively. Often, our communication is unclear, hazy, and inauthentic. One only needs a little experience in the working world and various personal relationships to realize the extreme absence of real communication. We must master the ability to communicate with one another, one interaction at a time.

In our experience of helping hundreds of leaders, executives, and entrepreneurs get what they want from their businesses, we've realized they have all had an incredible privilege. They have had access to professional help, added perspective, and education that helps them view themselves, their businesses, and the world around them through a different lens. They've agreed to come together and fight through controversial topics and challenges to make their organizations better. We love that this is the case, but the challenge is that this benefit is accessible to only a few. As a result, a whole population of people are missing out on life-changing experiences.

In this book, we will share the experiences, training, and education we walk our clients through every day. We believe the magic and privilege don't have to be relegated to one room and a handful of leaders. We're here to share the brilliant conversations and breakthroughs our clients experience and make them accessible and applicable for all.

Our lives leading up to this moment have been fraught with mistakes and filled with communication mishaps, just like yours. The good news is that we always have the choice to learn and do better. We're changing and evolving to better ourselves and pass on the lessons and failures we've experienced to everyone we encounter so that we all learn together. We've seen the work that follows leave huge impacts on the lives of hundreds of individuals. The beauty of it is that what works in their lives will also work in your own life. Why? Because at the end of the day we're all just humans who must communicate and build connections and relationships with other people in this world.

We've designed what follows for those who want to overcome the divides and learn to use real communication to benefit themselves and the rest of the world. This book is for those who want to experience greater peace and more space to be themselves. It is for those who want to truly know where they stand in each moment. It is for those who feel the growing disconnectedness between us and want to do something about it. And it is for those who intend to treat life as a gift.

2

Understanding Our Differences: *Imagine a World of Real Communication*

One of the greatest achievements we can ever attain is to be 100 percent ourselves. It all begins with the first step in real communication—*honesty*. Honesty starts from within. It starts with you and your choices to be or not to be who you are. A willingness and courage to state who you are, what you want, and how you feel. Said another way, be your authentic self. Being free is a tremendous feeling. And it's as close to living as you can be, with one glaring exception: You can't accomplish it alone because we aren't alone.

It's wonderful to be truly and freely ourselves. But what does that mean for the lives around us? To be completely honest would be easy if you lived on an island with no one to think of but yourself. That is not our reality. So, what happens when your honesty brushes against someone else's opposing honesty? Suddenly, we have a problem. If we stick with our own honesty, others may not like, love, or accept us. We've created friction by being ourselves because our honesty doesn't always align with others'. This can quickly cause division and a bit of discomfort. So, as with all powerful forces, honesty must have an equal and opposing partner to thrive. In a place shared with others, in a world where real communication needs to exist, honesty on its own is not enough. We also need the second half of real communication—*openness.*

When two people come together and create an expectation of real communication, what is spoken must also be received. Listeners can't receive vital information if there is no openness between the two of them. Thus, one half of our equation is honesty, and the other half is openness.

OPENNESS
+ HONESTY

REAL COMMUNICATION

In our work, we find that the best version of people is when they are the most honest. It's real, raw, vulnerable, and true. Without their honesty, we end up with a dangerous fantasy—a fake version of them. We can't do much with that. If we try to work with it, we end up chasing something insignificant and unnecessary. In other words, we must embrace honesty so we can make real progress.

Bringing more honesty into our lives requires us to consciously recognize the moments where we are and are *not* being honest. When we are in our best and highest state of mind, we lean into those moments of honesty. That makes us free. In fact, "freedom" is the most common feeling we hear associated with our clients bringing more openness and honesty into their lives. They feel like they can breathe easier, not have to second-guess what others are saying and release the need to control other people. We've seen toxic cultures transform into ones where everyone's ideas can be heard and respected.

Ken shares the transformation of his client Deksia:

Taming the Bulls

In 2019, three business owners were struggling to boost their marketing company, Deksia, to the next level. They were in a difficult spot, one that most entrepreneurs will experience at some point in their careers. Each of the owners was infused with passion and brought unique talents to the business. Aaron, the visionary, was outspoken and fearless about any topic. When challenged, he was always ready to pounce. At times, his approach was warranted, and at other times, completely unnecessary. JR, lead creative, was strong with opinions, always dreaming, and never short of ideas or a new angle. His statements were sometimes clear and other times hazy, even seemingly wacky. Conran, the CEO, was a bit more mild-mannered, although he, too, could be unwaveringly opinionated at times.

During my first day with them, I realized I was working with three bulls. Each was screwed up some-how, but I loved them for it. As this group worked through problems and planning, quite often, we needed to stop the process because of a conflict. And these were not typical business disagreements. Every interaction seemed to lead to a complete verbal assault.

Aaron would suggest an approach to the sales department, and Conran would dismiss it as unreasonable. Aaron would, in turn, dig into Conran and suggest he was stubborn. JR might chime in, looking to help, and suggest we look at it in a different way. What ensued was a cycle of attempts to disprove each person's approach. The more the cycle ran its course, the more frustrated each person became. Suggestions were made, then disapprovals, followed by some snide remarks. Onto the next suggestion, one would roll his eyes, the others groaned or remarked disapproval, and the cycle continued. The discussions began to take their toll as everyone's emotions flared. I always needed to end the cycle with "Let's take a five-to-seven-minute break" before the tensions boiled over.

As I found myself trapped in their cycle of disagreement and disapproval, I tried to pick up on what happened to this team. My thoughts went through hundreds of scenarios as to why they behaved this way. I wondered if this approach was their historical norm or just a blip of anger. What was the source of their painful communication? I needed to observe more, so I pressed on, facilitating the dysfunction.

Typically, when we returned from break, Aaron would bring some clarity to the debate. Sometimes, it would land, and other times, it would exhaust the team and restart the cycle. No matter the volatility of the argument, by the end of our time together, I was able to get the team to "agree" to a plan and course of action for their organization. But underneath that agreement, I could sense that none of them bought into it completely.

We'd meet every three months, and during our time together, I would try to get the team realigned in their "agreed-upon" direction. But each time they were walking into the session with similar results from a few months prior, so we had our work cut out for us yet again.

I would always start the sessions with a handful of rules, two of which were "Be honest" and "Be open." Occasionally, the rules would resonate with them. One might strike a chord, and at other times, they would all go in one ear and out the other. Regardless, I kept repeating those rules, hoping they would hear them.

Another three months later, I found myself back in the saddle with Deksia, but this time it was different. We had to conduct the session virtually due to government-imposed rules during the COVID-19 pandemic. Unfortunately, we were trapped on screens and had to get through a tough agenda. As we moved through issues and opportunities, the usual behaviors recurred. Someone would suggest a move, someone else would shoot it down, and the conversation would unravel from there.

We were back into our usual cycles. But this time, it spiraled. Aaron began using much more aggressive language. JR and Conran didn't seem rattled, and they engaged. Phrases like "stupid" this and "mother f-er" that, or "this is all BS," were exchanged between the three. I missed an important moment to relax the pressure with a break before it escalated. And there, right before our eyes, started a newer, nastier cycle in our session. We took the much-needed break, only to have the team return with a similar tone. The damage was done, and it was deep.

The session went over our stop time by two hours just so we could check a few boxes to get the bare minimum done. The team had a plan going forward, but no one had bought in. We all left that day feeling exhausted and incomplete. After our session, I made phone calls to all three. From each of the leaders' updates, it was clear the tension carried well into the next quarter. There were multiple suggestions of separating the company and doubts that the three could work together at all. It was looking like my bulls were ready to run in opposite directions. Or even worse, charge at one another.

I'll never forget my phone call with Aaron during this time. I knew we had to talk about the aggressive nature of what took place in the session. I asked him, "What was that? Is that something you were proud of?"

Despite the intense emotion of the situation, he said, "Of course not." We unpacked what had taken place. There were some important moments, in reflection, that Aaron didn't like about his approach. He recognized that he had been getting too emotional and flying off the handle. Even though he wasn't the only guilty party, he was certainly the primary fire starter. He wasn't proud of how he carried himself with his team. It was out of character. He didn't like the interaction and clearly had acted from a place of emotion and pain. I ended our conversation with, "I know brilliant Aaron, and I love brilliant Aaron. I want more moments of brilliance from you and far fewer moments of that garbage from back there."

From those phone calls, serious conversations took place between the team about what they were going to do with ownership and whether they were able to continue working together. Ultimately, and largely due to Conran's ability to navigate challenges like these, the three decided to keep the company together. That decision led to more meetings and sessions together. But something special happened the next time we connected. During our next session, Aaron had one of the most brilliant moments I've seen from a leader to date. The team was stuck on their long-term target. No one believed in the unrealistic trajectory set forth. I could feel that we were on the precipice of one of their senseless cycles of disagreement and disapproval.

But this time Aaron wouldn't settle for less, nor let his team believe in less. He challenged the team with the following statement: "I don't want to hear 'We can't do this,' or 'We can't do that.' I only want to hear 'We can if....'" He wanted his team to paint their own picture of how. He wanted to hear, "We could make these growth projections if we ___." Not only was this statement profound, but the approach was not one the team had previously considered or attempted.

Aaron chose to leave his offensive post and allow others to have the floor. He embraced an open approach. In the moment of the team exploring "We can if...," their ideas were finally being heard, ridiculous or not. JR's wacky ideas were being met with more acceptance and curiosity. Conran was validated for his concerns.

From that moment forward, they created a bold plan they all believed in. They could finally buy into it because they were all being heard and understood. They were affirming each other. They had always been good at being honest—brutally honest at times—but they hadn't pushed on to the other side of real communication: being open. Now, they were open to one another's views, perspectives, and thoughts. They had cracked the code of real communication, and a whole new fire was lit within Deksia. The more they leaned into being open, the more they became a real team. They began improving and communicating better than ever before.

Deksia has gone on to have growth rates much higher than industry norms. Their increase in the bottom line was the most they had experienced in their company's lifetime. Their culture was desirable in the marketplace, in turn making recruiting simple. They made real progress on major company challenges. Because of their newfound ability to communicate, they solved problems quickly, giving everyone a voice that could be heard. They have become a shining example of open and honest communication making a huge positive impact in an organization. They learned an important lesson: the quickest way to cultivate more honesty is to allow others to express theirs.

The more you can release the need to control a situation, the more freedom you will experience. You begin freeing up the space for everyone else and, in turn, also make more space for yourself. Deksia's previous approach of disagreement and disapproval didn't leave room for anyone else. And because of it, the team was missing. Listening without reservation to the collective honesty gave them speed. Honesty gave them truth and uncovered the real issues to solve quickly. Without a commitment to real communication, they would have faced false challenges with solutions that wouldn't move them forward. Honesty clarified the problem, and openness made a solution possible, ultimately making progress easier.

Because we share this world, we cannot walk through it expecting to only project our honesty. We're missing the vital exchange—others receiving our honesty *and* having room to share theirs. This constant exchange of openness and honesty creates freedom for you and those around you. It enhances understanding, connection, belonging, and happiness. We hope, at this point, it's becoming apparent that these are skills we need to understand and practice. Something bigger and better is brewing for all of us.

From our experiences, honesty tends to be the easier part of the equation. We frequently and actively drop the ball on the other half of real communication: openness. It's difficult to be open when the other person doesn't share our same interest or viewpoint. We've gotten lazy and selfish, and we lack the discipline to focus on others. That's what holds us back. It is so much easier to disagree or simply ignore someone than try to understand. It is easier to disconnect than spend the time and energy to truly hear what is being said.

But what if we could flip this scenario?
What if we were able to be both open and honest?
What would such a world be like?

If our world was transformed with honesty:

- dating couples would engage in more transparency, experiencing clarity on who is really in front of them;

- coworkers would communicate challenges they previously held back, helping to identify problems quickly;

- patients would tell doctors their true medical concerns, resulting in better healthcare and targeting the right ailments;

- citizens would know who they are really voting for and create a fairer government;

- spouses would share grievances sooner and resolve them before they grew into resentment, creating happier marriages;

- customers would be clearer about complaints and inform organizations of their real issues;

- conversations would have real feelings and desires expressed, creating more meaningful moments of connection.

If we transformed our world with openness, listening without reservation:

- dating couples would be less critical about differences, giving more potential relationships a chance to succeed;
- coworkers who disagree would hear each other out, resulting in quality solutions and collaboration;
- patients would be more understanding of medical staff, easing stresses between patient-provider relations;
- opposing political views would become more heard and understood, reviving bipartisanship and civil discourse;
- spouses would remove judgment from their listening, creating deeper partnerships;
- customers would be more understanding of product and service mishaps, reducing angst;
- conversations would become less about personal agendas and more about the relationship.

When we entered this shared world, we were thrust into a world divided. We were given the gift of communication, only to be taught by the world how to do it all wrong. We recreated what others had modeled for us without any intentional thought or reflection on whether it was helpful. But a beautiful fact about human beings is our unceasing ability to adapt and explore. We are waking up to the old, broken models of communication. We are realizing that we are capable of changing how the world communicates for the better.

Dream a little bigger with us for a moment: If the entire population agreed to be more open and honest, we'd have a chance at greater world peace. That is a huge claim, but the root of our issues is simple. We are not both open and honest with one another. This idea of greater peace between people is not out of reach; it's right there in front of us. The choice to be honest and the choice to be open are built-in options in each exchange we have with every person who crosses our path.

Creating an "Unimaginable" World

We know that communication is the key to doing better together, but as you can see, we still haven't got it right. We've taken our God-given gifts and used them to create a false reality. We've made tools to claim we are now connected worldwide, yet it feels like we are more disconnected than ever before.

We need to open our eyes. We are shutting out each other and our differences, technologically, psychologically, and verbally. We take everyday opportunities for connection and miss them completely.

Our differences are not an obstacle to overcome. Rather, they are part of what creates the true condition in the first place. Differences are here to

We've made tools to claim we are now connected worldwide, yet it feels like we are more disconnected than ever before.

stay. When we recognize how we differ from another person, we often decide to distance ourselves and build a barrier between us to avoid any possible conflict. This is a horrible default habit, and it's not helping us; it's hurting us.

As we continually distance ourselves, we lose a vital part of what makes us human. We thrive and rely on connection and belonging. It is part of the equation to live a happier, more fulfilling life. As Dr. Brené Brown says, "Connection is why we're here; it is what gives purpose and meaning to our lives."[1] By creating barriers between ourselves and others, we lose out on much of the beauty of life. We tend to see all the differences as a negative, not as a positive.

We've developed an ugly, self-centered mindset, creating calluses that build up over time until we become so hardened and disoriented that we fail to realize our own humanity reflected back to us by those around us. We are now rejecting the reality we live in—one with conflicts, disagreements, and friction—and crippling our ability to connect.

It is our reservations, fears, and judgments of others that ruin relationships. Rather than having a conversation to clarify what someone meant by a previous statement or where they stand on an issue, we remain steadfast and unwilling to understand what events and experiences in their own life led them to such a conclusion. We then parse that individual down to a caricature based on one or two controversial opinions they hold. Then, we begin to disconnect from them. We continue minimizing that person until even the mention of their name elicits eye rolls and frustration. The issue of disconnection and misunderstanding persists. Our minds will continue to view that individual and relationship in a negative light until we choose to resolve it.

This begs the question: How long are we willing to let the disconnect remain until we take action? It will not go away. Will we simply tolerate that relationship moving forward or make the choice to change it for the better? In not addressing the initial disconnect, we remain in a state of ambiguity where each conversation leaves us frustrated and disgruntled. But you have a choice. You can choose to put aside the preconceived notions and engage to see them as a complex human being, just as you are.

Imagine if we had the courage to bring our full selves to the table *and* invite everyone else to do the same. It is an alternative where you get to be heard, understood, and able to enjoy the space to be truly and freely you without judgment or expectations, *and* everyone else at the table enjoys that same freedom too. That is the table to which we are inviting you. Together, we can create real relationships and a world in which each one of us thrives.

Together, we can create real relationships and a world in which each one of us thrives.

It's about bringing to the table the good, the bad, the ugly, and otherwise, and being able to talk about all of it freely. To experience the true condition in such a way is to accept the clarity that has the potential to set us all free. Imagine the world we could create if we chose not to distance ourselves from each other. One where we knew each person's thoughts and opinions, and we could get a clearer picture of what we're dealing with in all facets of life. A world in which, in lieu of distance, we instead chose connection. We want that table for our personal relationships, our working relationships, for everyone.

Ken shares a story about his personal relationships:

Perhaps the best example I can think of is connecting with my children and wife at the dinner table. We have the potential to create the most real, intimate, important conversations together. We could discuss our days and connect with one another, releasing our stresses, laughing and learning together. We would have meaningful exchanges. Yes, we can connect; the potential is there. But the reality is that in my family, we rarely choose to do so. The television will often be playing in the background. I find myself scrolling on my phone, reading emails, or looking at the next podcast I want to download. More likely than not, both kids will bring an iPad to the table. At times, one of us leaves dinner early for another more entertaining activity. Disconnectedness, aided by technology, can take over in an instant. And it often does.

Throughout our work, we've learned that we are not the only ones to do this. It's happening in our personal and professional worlds. One of our client's executive teams was working through the financial losses of their small business.

The business owner was hesitant to share how bad the losses were, and the other team members feared the conversation about to take place. Just before we were about to dive in, the owner took out his phone and started thumbing away, looking for a nonessential cellular distraction.

In that crucial moment, he immediately disconnected. Team members sat in unnecessary anticipation. The owner continued thumbing on as if no one else was there. We took that moment to remind him that we were the six most important people in the room until our session ended and that we had an important topic to address. We then asked him to put away the phone and keep his attention on the people in the room.

Thankfully, he obliged. But it wasn't just the technology that disconnected us. It was the avoidance that ensued. The owner shared the financial picture, but not all of it. He didn't share how scared he was for the business. He didn't share how embarrassed he was to let it get this far. He didn't share that he really needed help. He missed an opportunity to let his team in, and he certainly failed to expose the true condition. He wasn't honest about how he truly felt, and his face exposed that dishonesty. The team members sat in silence, not engaging in the presented information. They were holding back, too. Despite our encouragement and a series of questions, the team didn't take it any deeper. A quarter went by, and the losses persisted.

When the team came together for the next meeting, the financials were still not trending in a positive direction. The owner persisted in similar avoidance. Familiar silence came from the other team members until one woman spoke up and asked, "How bad is it? I mean, really, how bad is it?" She was thinking about it the whole time, but finally, she found the courage to share it aloud. Now, we were getting somewhere! The owner reluctantly shared the financials and bared his soul. He shared his fears and let it all out. He let the team in on his emotional state and dropped all the walls. We watched as the team transformed.

In that moment, and because this woman helped knock down the barriers to communication, they became engaged, asking questions, suggesting, commenting, and contributing. Real communication was now on the table, and we were able to make progress. We talked through the legitimate issues, opinions, and perspectives from everyone in the group. Leaving that meeting, everyone was finally fully informed and able to execute a plan to turn this sinking ship around. As they filed out of that conference room, you could feel a sense of relief and renewed purpose. Exposing the true condition had set the team free.

That interaction proved to make a huge difference. The company began to turn results around in the next three quarters. They eventually moved on to have record earnings and record years—all because they chose to engage. They entered the uncomfortable together and shared what was on their minds. Now, they have a successful business and a thriving work environment for everyone.

Sadly, such a fairytale-like ending is not always the case. We've seen plenty of instances where the outcomes are not so positive. Those turning moments drove us to do this work. We have seen what disconnection does to people. These stories in our personal and work lives take place all the time. Right now, it is normal to disconnect and create division. And, even more concerning, it's become acceptable. This negative approach cripples relationships of all types and organizations in all industries.

Having technology at our fingertips greatly accelerates the disconnect between us. Staring at a screen is much easier than looking someone in the eye and having a difficult conversation, so we often choose the path of least resistance and let the disconnection remain. But we are social creatures, and we rely upon connection. Taking the easy way out robs families and relationships of meaningful connections and organizations of transformational results.

But we can't blame it all on technology. Our words and body language serve as drivers for disconnection too. Crossing our arms, rolling our eyes, or closing off our bodies to others make it clear we're not interested in engaging. When we use our words like daggers or talk down to people, we distance ourselves and deepen our disconnection. If we habitually use any of these drivers of disconnection, we cannot be surprised when we find ourselves among the 61 percent of adults who "report that they sometimes or always feel lonely," as found by the Cigna US Loneliness Index.[2] That number only increases as we look at younger generations, pointing to a problem we must fix today for the sake of tomorrow. Connection is fully within our reach, and communication is the greatest tool at our disposal.

Meaningful Change Is Within Reach

Given the stories above, please make this important note: If you intend to make a change and implement the lessons contained herein, you must own it. Ponder it. It *is* a choice. Your choice is to engage or disengage. Your choice is to accept relationships or deny them. Your choice is to be who you truly are or let the whims of society drag you into someone you are not. Your choice is to give people the space to shine as they are or shut them out. Right now, we are choosing to stay disconnected. We are choosing short-term, meaningless gain over long-term, meaningful happiness. We are taking the easier path out. Our choices butcher the one life we have and rob the lives we share with others. It's ripping progress out of our hands, and it's killing us.

Each story we've told so far takes place millions of times, again and again, all over the world. And each moment comes with a choice. We can truly and freely be ourselves. We can state how we feel and speak into what we want. We can let others in. We can give others space to be who they are. We can listen without reservation. We can put our needs and wants on pause for others. But if we don't, we lose as a society.

Less Control, More Life

Our brains act as machines designed to embrace efficiency and routines, driving a strong desire for control. But what do we miss when we ride out life on these automatic responses? What becomes unseen or misunderstood because the blinders are on? When we live our lives unexamined and without curiosity, we're actually missing out on life. We're favoring isolation, false realities, and control. We're not eliminating enough walls to experience the life we've been gifted. We're not becoming an open human race; we're becoming a closed one.

It's easy to believe we are in control of all aspects of our lives, but that is hardly the case. We are driving ourselves crazy, believing control is what

> When we live our lives unexamined and without curiosity, we're actually missing out on life.

sets us free. We have little influence over China's import policies, what the new flavor of M&Ms will be, or even if our neighbor will ever mow their lawn. We build walls with no foundation to block out what we don't like or agree with. We, knowingly or not, try to control other people, thinking we will magically change the outcomes in our favor. We're driving ourselves deeper into stress, anxiety, and anger while other people have no idea they're involved in our turmoil.

Here's the little secret about this control that we so desperately want: *absolute control isn't attainable because it doesn't exist.*

We cannot write a magic code that will allow us to fully control another human being. Parents raising kids live this lesson every day. Bosses leading teams of people know this as well. Teachers and professors know this, people sharing public transportation know this, and we live this lesson repeatedly.

Absolute control isn't attainable because it doesn't exist.

You see, we live it, but the lesson doesn't stick. There is a grand absence of education out there. This is not taught enough in the classroom or the boardroom, certainly not in grade schools, and rarely in the business community. If anything, the opposite is learned. We are told if we work hard enough, then we can control every time, outcome, person, or particular objective. We are driving ourselves to madness. We need less of this obsessive need to control everyone and everything and more of us putting our needs and wants on pause for someone else.

We want so badly to live in the land of our own making. Yet, it is simply impossible. What is possible is to release our need for control. We can learn to be open to the other souls walking beside us in this life. We can learn to love other people's journeys instead of bulldozing everyone else. We can let them be truly and freely themselves.

Every living person adds to the complexity of the external world around us. The smallest events, even halfway around the world, have the grandest of impacts on the masses. With billions of scenarios and experiences crashing into one another, it's undeniable that this world is tethered to all who live in it. Don't let the thought overwhelm you; instead embrace it. Admire the beauty that can be formed from this interconnectedness. It's a special design, and we must navigate it in a way that enhances the outcomes for everyone.

You can let this interconnectedness frustrate you, or you can accept that this is just the way of the world. No matter your attitude or perception, the reality of it doesn't change. Knowing the rules of the game and building your skills give you an advantage in how you play it. You have an opportunity to better navigate this life and all its complexities. If we can understand that our ability to be truly and freely ourselves is directly correlated to our ability to allow others to be truly and freely themselves, then can we achieve an extraordinary togetherness. When you give that freedom to others, you will better experience it for yourself. When you encourage someone to be themselves, you build a space to be yourself. You put up fewer expectations, guardrails, and judgments and free up space for everyone. You reduce the difficulty.

We have the capability to communicate with brilliance and grace. We could give our precise thoughts, exact feelings, and opinions, yet we don't. We could hear someone's journey and show interest and respect, yet we won't. Frankly, no one delivers or participates in real communication 100 percent of the time. Professor Frey is right—communication is the biggest issue companies face. And it is the single biggest issue our society faces. We have made communication seem confusing, frustrating, and complex. But it is also our path toward more freedom, peace, and confidence.

We must put our needs and wants on pause for those we share this world with. When you better achieve openness and put yourself second, you then accelerate your understanding of others. You bring more reality into the conversation, remove the guesswork, form genuine relationships, and ultimately create real communication, the purest level possible. We are primed for this work. We have the tools and resources to make a lasting change in our world together. Now is the time to master the skills and create a culture of real communication—to create openness and know honesty.

Let's begin with honesty.

3

Essentials of Honesty: *The Beginning of Real Communication*

H ow are you?

We'd bet a sizable amount of money that your first thought was either "good," "fine," or "busy."

We've gotten into our habitual responses when asked questions like this one. When was the last time you answered that question with full honesty? Did you take a moment to think about your life, your health, or your passions? Are you even willing to be who you truly are? And when we ask this question of others, do we expect or want an honest response? Or have we fallen into a way of communicating that perpetuates fakeness?

Over one-fourth of the communication that leaves our mouth is not honest. We've calculated this number after measuring hundreds of people's honesty through The Pursuit of Honesty® Assessment (more on this in Chapter 8). We're guilty of this, as are you and the other eight billion people in this world. We all lack total honesty. It has become an epidemic, but it doesn't have to be this way. We can find a path to honesty, one where we all benefit.

We chose to work with organizations because at their core are people and because of that, the foundational source of all their problems boils down to a lack of open and honest communication. After spending most of our careers in this sphere, it became clear that this single issue was holding back the business world.

Early on in our journey, we gave a presentation to a group of business consultants. We had them complete this exercise: "Name a time when one of your clients was not honest, and it hurt the company. Then share with the person to your left." They all quickly exploded in dialogue. A room full of consultants shared their many reasons why a lack of honesty in various industries hurt their clients' organizations. We felt the overwhelming vibration and buzz in the room as they explained and commiserated with one another. Clearly, we were not the only ones seeing the lack of honesty. We all had experienced it—a shared pain point that was all too common for those helping people across every profession and industry.

When working with clients, much of our effort is getting different people to work out their disagreements and align their perspectives on a common objective. To increase the likelihood that our relationships are open and honest and engaged in real communication, several factors must be present:

1. We must agree to be in a safe environment that promotes free-flowing communication.

2. The client must be educated on and embrace the importance of being open and honest, repeatedly.

3. We must be on our game, present and ready to facilitate anything and everything that makes its way to the table.

Once these rules are in place, we bring in real communication and set it free. Throughout our time together, we'll see themes of these three factors surfacing. So, for now, keep them in your back pocket to serve real communication and your relationships.

We'd like to ask you the same question we ask the teams in our session room: "If we can't be honest with each other, what are we being? If you can't be freely and truly you in this room, then who are you?"

Think about this for a moment. Who are you when you're not being truly and freely yourself?

Our clients quickly respond to this question with words such as *fraud*, *phony*, and, our favorite answer, *fake*. The short answer is that you are not being yourself, and it shows. When we choose to be fake, we cast confusion into everyone's life. It is not self-serving. It is self-harming. When clients are not honest, we end up solving fake issues. They chase down solutions to problems that aren't clear because someone skirted the truth or wasn't being sincere about the condition of the problem.

Other times, clients pretend to be agreeable when they don't agree at all. And when that team comes together to create a vision for their organization without their honest input, the vision becomes less meaningful, and individuals are less committed to it because they didn't speak up. The bottom line is that if people can't be honest, they have little hope of achieving what they actually want.

Many clients have challenged us with the "what ifs." They will question specific scenarios, trying to prove that honesty's value is worthless or unrealistic. It's fascinating to see the lengths to which a person's imagination will go to challenge honesty, almost as if they would rather continue living blind to its value in our world and remain in dishonesty. We assure you less honesty creates more chaos and discontent than anything else. At the time of this publication, we are seeing and tracking a positive correlation between an increase in honesty and an increase in life satisfaction.

Simplifying the Honesty Side of Communication

As we researched and tested many iterations of the definitions, we concluded that, as a society, we lacked a *clear, simple,* and *relatable* definition. Here is our definition: Honesty is being truly and freely yourself, speaking into what you want and how you feel.

Honesty does not have to be complicated or foreign. It exists in you already; it is a matter of scaling and growing its presence and relevance in your life. To make honesty most effective, let's keep it simple. Absorb the above definition and these essentials below to begin to move your levels of honesty higher.

Honesty is being truly and freely yourself, speaking into what you want and how you feel.

The Three Essentials of Honesty are:

- Truly and Freely You™
- True Condition
- About You

Let's round out our understanding of what it means to be honest, understand the definition to its fullest extent, and unpack each essential.

The First Essential: Truly and Freely You™

This is the first essential by design because it serves as the foundation for the next two. How do you know if you're being truly and freely you? We encourage you to pause, take a breath, relax your shoulders, settle your stress, and sit with who you are in the moment.

When you're able to be truly and freely yourself around others and be well received, it will feel like a breath of fresh air. Over time, by growing your honesty, you will learn to express yourself with ease, even in the presence of resistance. Too often, we try to live for others by pleasing people and saying things we don't really mean to avoid friction or conflict. That is not a breath of fresh air. That is like inhaling smoke or putting plastic over your mouth. It's not recommended. Being truly and freely you means being comfortable in your own skin, no matter the scenario. It is existing as you are, with the values you hold, doing and knowing what matters most to you. It is letting your freak flag fly, regardless of others' opinions. It is just you being unapologetically you.

Gino Wickman, founder of EOS® Worldwide, visionary, author, and good friend, learned firsthand the feeling of not being truly and freely himself. He shares this story from his books *The EOS Life* and *Shine*:

Have you ever felt you are one person at work, one person at home, one person out with your friends, and so on? You're trying to be all things to all people. The textbook example of this happened when my wife threw me a surprise 30th birthday party. When I saw 100 people yell, "Surprise!" I was first excited, then struck by a sinking feeling of "Holy cow! Who am I going to be today?"

That's because I could see six different factions of my life in one room.

There were my employees and business partners. My family—mom, dad, brothers, and cousins. My wife's family. My high school friends. My entrepreneur friends, and friends from the neighborhood.

I realized I was literally a different person with each of these six groups of people.

With my employees, I was "boss Gino." With my high school friends, I was "crazy Gino." With my new friends I was "less-crazy Gino." And so on.

It was a wake-up call, and from that day on I was "authentic Gino."

Imagine the energy I was expending being who I felt I had to be with each individual group.

Now, I am simply myself with everyone. I am hardworking, hard-playing, passionate, intense, beer-drinking, obsessive, introverted, gritty me. And being that way makes me feel a thousand pounds lighter.

Being someone you are not saps your energy.

If you are anything like us, or Gino, or the hundreds of people we work with, then you, too, likely spend too much time worrying about what others think of you. This causes a lack of confidence in yourself and creates an "I am not enough as I am" mentality. The actions we take are often influenced by someone else rather than considering what it is we truly want. How can we value our individual uniqueness when hundreds, if not thousands, of people in our lives, tell us to be who we are not? It can feel like an uphill battle. But if we can agree to embrace our own honesty and those around us, we will shift societal trends.

When it comes to our work lives, we see clients struggle with employees who are not a good fit in their organization. The personality of the employee often directly conflicts with the culture these leaders want to cultivate. Instead of forcing their employees to conform, we encourage them to give opportunities for behavior changes and adjustment. It's not going to work out if they won't change or don't want to. When that is the case, it's best to release the employee's talents back into the workforce and let them find a better match for themselves. You've done your organization and the people in it a favor.

The organization hired the wrong fit, and the employee chose the wrong company. Both parties always do better when they are matched with the people and places where they can be truly and freely themselves. To spend our time in places and doing work that doesn't align with who we are saps our energy and ensures we're never giving our best efforts to the organization. It wastes our talents, company resources, and the precious time we have on this earth.

You are the only you in this world. There is no cause, need, or want worth the cost of devaluing yourself. Going down that path is a guaranteed method to end up hating your life. It is a waste of energy that you could be using toward your goals and really getting what you want out of this one precious life. It takes knowing, understanding, and a healthy dose of self-love to believe you are enough as you are to be truly and freely you.

To live with greater honesty, let's speak into what we want and how we feel. We begin to attach desires and goals that align with who we really are more easily. We can pursue them with more clarity and conviction.

Consider what holds you back from being 100 percent truly and freely you. A few real-life examples:

- trying to maintain friendships that have different expectations than you
- having a strong desire to please everyone and fit into all scenarios
- being fearful of expressing your concerns at work, so you say nothing
- staying quiet or skirting the truth around certain family members who don't value you
- being unclear on who you really are

The common thread is that we all are afraid of being ostracized for simply being ourselves. And so, rather than feel that freedom, we hide behind a façade that doesn't allow us to show how we really think and feel. Fear holds each one of us back and, therefore, holds all of us back.

You step into who you truly and freely are when you don't hold back. You show up in a way that represents who you really are at your natural state of being. When you choose this path, life feels more fluid, almost easy. At this higher, more aligned state of mind, your confidence soars, along with your willingness to step out and get what you really want in life. That breath of fresh air comes from no longer living within the boundaries of everyone else's expectations.

Take a moment to think about who you truly and freely are. Better yet, write it down.

1. What matters most to you in life?

2. What makes you, *you*?

3. What brings you down?

4. What brings you up?

5. Where are your talents and abilities best put to use?

Recognizing the unique value you bring to this world takes time. There is no one else out there like you, with all the experiences and lessons contained within you. You are unique. Bring your value, perspective, and desire to this world. Be truly and freely you.

The Second Essential: True Condition

With the foundation of being truly and freely you, we move into understanding the second essential: true condition. This is less about the feeling and more about accepting the facts and reality around you. The true condition requires everyone's honesty. By leaning into who you really are, you better articulate and share the facts and reality.

Sometimes, we avoid what is truly happening in our lives. Perhaps you disagree with someone but don't share your opinion, therefore appearing as if you agree. Not sharing your honesty may keep the peace momentarily, but it does not uncover the conflict and impedes progress. It will leave you with a level of tension and fakeness within yourself and in the relationship until the conflict is discussed. As long as the true condition remains hidden, the division between you and others will persist.

When we refuse to express how we're really doing, feeling, or thinking, we rob everyone of access to the true condition. An opportunity for connection and a real relationship is missed. Even if our honest answer is simply "I don't know," that gives others a clearer understanding than saying nothing. Not offering our honesty becomes a block when we attempt to solve conflicts and disrupts our ability to collectively do better together.

Ken shares the following example:

I was working with a team that had a new human resources professional named Cassie. We began discussing the lessons learned from the previous quarter. One of the major topics was the lack of recruits coming in. On top of that, the company was experiencing some serious retention issues. As the dialogue continued, Cassie became more and more visibly upset but remained silent and gave little input. As we continued, it became apparent that the source of the issues rested in HR. We directed the questions and discussion toward Cassie. At that moment, she erupted in tears.

I had the team take a break to let Cassie collect her thoughts and reconvene. Working through the tears, she told the team how it was hard to handle the incoming volume of applicants. She went on to say how frustrated she was with the lack of support in following the processes she put in place. Lastly, she felt her team wasn't granted the appropriate resources to do their job well. Cassie had held herself back for months, holding on to how she really felt rather than sharing it. But once she let it all out, the team finally had access to the true condition of the recruiting issue. They could finally see the full picture. Cassie freed herself of that burden and gave the team and organization much-needed clarity.

As the session went on, the team addressed those immediate issues. Because Cassie had expressed herself clearly, the team solved what was really standing in their way. Everyone spoke directly to the issues and to each other. Cassie accepted the severity and addressed it in a way the team should have been several quarters prior.

Cassie's delay in being honest about her thoughts had set the company back months. But now that she found her courage to be truly and freely herself, and share the true condition, the company could finally forge ahead. Without access to the true condition, that key missing piece of Cassie's honesty, this company would have been on the hamster wheel for many more months. If you don't have the true condition, you'll find it nearly impossible to progress. And this doesn't just happen within organizations and leadership teams; it happens in our personal lives too.

Consider this story from Grace:

"Yeah, I never understood what you saw in him," she said so casually. I was shocked to hear my other friends chime in agreement.

"Then why didn't any of you *say* anything?" I burst out.

In my younger years, I spent too much time in a relationship that everyone around me knew was not the right match. I eventually figured it out, too, but only after repeated wonderings and considering if I was making the right decision. After all, I didn't want to be the "bad guy" and hurt someone's feelings. There was nothing so terribly wrong with this person, but our values and life trajectories were not aligned, and, ultimately, there was no spark. When I thought deeply about my life and what I wanted out of it, this person simply didn't fit. But to uncover and embrace that fact—and then do something about it—are two very different actions.

I had my perspective on the relationship, but I was missing what could only be seen from the outside of it. I questioned myself about my decision: Am I missing something? Maybe this is all I should expect out of a relationship. Objectively, it's okay, but is life about settling for what's just okay? If one person in my life had stepped up and called out the mismatch with loving honesty, I would have had more clarity and confidence to move forward sooner and end the relationship. Instead, it dragged on, which made parting all the more difficult. It was only afterward that the doubts and confusion surfaced.

Why is it that only when a relationship ends do all the people around us come forward with their honesty? We watch from afar and wonder what it is our loved one sees in their partner. Rarely will people ask the difficult questions or point out what they are seeing, even though that's how they feel. Knowing that we struggle to see the true condition for ourselves, who will help us get access to it? We need people in our lives who also subscribe to being honest. Without them and our own commitment to embrace the true condition, we end up making more critical errors in our own lives.

This resistance to the true condition plays out again and again in our personal and work lives. Take, for instance, individuals who are too insecure or uncomfortable to bring forth an issue at work. What if it was about a potentially toxic employee? Because we avoid the true condition, that toxic person remains at the organization for far too long, wreaking havoc on the culture and morale along the way. Or worse, management knows the situation, does nothing about it, and great employees leave. We shouldn't be scratching our heads asking why; we should realize our inability to access the true condition creates a series of problems for the foreseeable future. But if one individual is brave enough to be honest with their leadership, and that leader is open to hearing it, the toxicity can be dealt with much quicker, and the organization is better for it.

Knowing the true condition is central to your ability to get what you want. Without that, what are we working on? What are we chasing, seeking, or learning if we aren't basing it on the true condition? We need to know the true condition to accelerate any progress in business, relationships, problem-solving, and life in general.

The closer we are to 100 percent honesty, the clearer and more actionable life becomes. Knowing the true condition eliminates the messy guesswork and allows us and others to evolve. Honesty is a choice within our relationships, and should we make the right choice, it will be easier for everyone to navigate this complex world together.

The Third Essential: About You

Who are you?

We are not interested in who everyone thinks you are. We want you as you are.

So, who are you?

To give you a simple answer, you are who you are at this exact moment. The version of yourself that you are today—your feelings, your beliefs, your status, your impact, your demeanor, and the thousand other things that connect to you. That is the core of the third essential of honesty: about you. If it isn't clear yet, honesty isn't about what others think or feel. It's about you. Honesty starts with you and where you are in this moment.

Only you can share your honesty, and only you know what is really going on within your own heart and soul. You are the one who decides if your mind and your mouth will say the same things. When you have the courage to be you and share yourself with others, everything about you begins to make more sense for you and for those around you.

Ken shares this experience:

A friend of mine went through marriage counseling after struggling with some seriously misaligned expectations. He wasn't sharing his honesty, what he was frustrated with, how he felt, or what he needed out of the marriage. Neither was she. They weren't willing to express themselves and evaluate who they were and what they wanted. Instead, they forged ahead without addressing the hardships, needs, or wants, and the two grew apart.

As time went on, neither chose to be vulnerable, state what they needed from the marriage, or make it about themselves, even for just a moment. They chose to remain guarded. They had become convinced this was the easier way, even as their relationship deteriorated. Perhaps it might have been salvageable had they pivoted toward honesty, but when each chose to hide their wants and needs and avoid the issues, the relationship no longer stood a chance.

The best versions of themselves were no longer showing up in their marriage. Instead of being problem solvers, they became problem hiders. They existed in a way that allowed unspoken disagreements to fester and create a deeper divide between them.

Ultimately, the two divorced. It was one of the saddest times my friend ever faced. He had never expected this to happen in his life. I love my friend, I had cared about the health of his marriage, and I've grown to hate the hurt he went through in the process. A lot of that hurt is repairable, but it might have been avoided altogether by each partner remaining true to themselves throughout the relationship.

Many times, our thoughts and feelings come out of our mouths heavily filtered, leaving us unclear to the outer world. The reasons for the filters vary, from wanting to fit in to not feeling safe, to being unsure of how the other person will react, to falsely believing it's just easier that way. But every time you choose to filter yourself, the world loses a unique part of you. The closer you are to being unfiltered, the closer to 100 percent *you* is being shared, and the better off we all are for it.

One honesty trap we can fall into is when someone else shares our honesty rather than sharing it ourselves. Only you can give your honesty with the exact tone, words, and meaning you give it. Please don't expect anyone else to do it for you. When that happens, someone runs with it, and it becomes distorted, interrupting the natural flow of communication. It often comes out in the form of gossip and whispers that leave it prey to confusion and misconstruction. It is simply not your honesty; it's someone's interpretation of your honesty.

A few professions, including lawyers, priests, therapists, and coaches, do an exceptional job of not sharing their clients' honesty. They create a space in which the individual feels safe enough to share the darkest parts of themselves, knowing that it will not go beyond that room. In doing so, a connection is formed, and the individual has an opportunity to be deeply seen and heard.

Here is an example from Grace:

When I first began working with our executive coach, Aaron Einfeld, he asked me, "Throughout our time together, what would you feel comfortable with me sharing with Ken if he asks?" At this point, Aaron had been working with Ken for several months, and we all had formed a strong relationship. I was grateful he brought this topic to the table, as I had yet to consider that scenario. He wanted to ensure I felt comfortable in the space to share and explore together.

"For me, I'd prefer you send Ken my way to ask that question. It's not that I have anything to hide, but if we uncover a tough conversation or pivot that needs to be shared, I'd rather the message be delivered from me so that the two of us can keep the communication going," I replied. Aaron nodded his head, and we got to work.

And in my personal life, no one does a better job of not sharing another person's honesty than my husband, Eric. When a friend shares with him and asks that he not tell anyone else, he takes that promise seriously. No amount of begging or pleading on my end would get him to release that information. And while it deeply frustrated me in the past, I thoroughly respect him for it today.

When I asked him why he was committed to this, he said, "Trustworthiness is a two-way street. I don't want to be the one talking about what others aren't ready to share yet, just as I wouldn't want anyone doing that to me. I want to be the person that people can come to when they just need someone to listen. Because I don't share the small things about others, people share the big things with me rather than just keeping it to themselves. And I want my friends to be able to share. I don't want them going through a hard time and feeling like they have no one to talk to about it. Overall, I think it makes me a better friend and is a stepping stone to trust." Keeping what you share to only be about you guarantees it remains as clear as possible and allows others to share their honesty within real relationships when they are ready.

When what was shared in private becomes public through retelling someone else's honesty, not only is the trust within that relationship broken, but that individual, too, becomes less trustworthy. Keep this in mind when asking another person to be honest with you. It is your responsibility to create the space for honesty. If they share a conflict or struggle they're having with someone else, that is not yours to share. Rather than taking it upon yourself to involve the third party, encourage that person to continue the honesty and go discuss the conflict.

When you decide to be you through your honesty, you give the world the opportunity to understand you. The more *you* that shines through, the more you can match your needs and wants to the rest of the world. Your relationships will deepen because the person who chooses to be with you knows and accepts the real you. Your work will be better aligned with your vision and values. Your disagreements can be heard and have a chance to be resolved. Your desires become clear, creating a path to your future.

You being you is one of the greatest achievements you'll ever reach in your life. These three essentials of honesty are so simple yet remarkably powerful:

1. Truly and Freely You™
2. True Condition
3. About You

As you focus your life to ensure you keep each of these front and center, it is inevitable that you will peel back your protective layers and shed the fear of being completely honest in who you are and how you present yourself to the world. You'll strengthen your skill of honesty and be able to be truly and freely yourself, speaking into what you want and how you feel.

A Falter in Honesty

As you work toward more honesty in your life, inevitably, there will be times when you falter. You may act in ways that are out of line with who you really are and where you want your life and relationships to go. We all have random outbursts and emotional flare-ups or find ourselves in extraordinarily difficult circumstances. We say or do things that don't align with who we truly are. We often regret these moments and wish we could have a do-over.

This sense of regret surfaces because our actions or words aren't in alignment with who we believe ourselves to be. We all have a foundation of who we truly and freely are, as discussed in the first essential of honesty. Yet, at times, we lose touch with ourselves.

There are scenarios in which your mind and emotions give off the wrong intention, derailing honesty and separating you from yourself in the moment. If you're regularly unable to calmly and clearly express your honesty, you will encounter challenges on your path to getting what you really want and engaging in real relationships. Instead, return to who you are at your core. Take the time to be balanced there and in tune with yourself.

It's best to be centered around who you are and how you truly feel before blurting out whatever charged emotion emerges first. In heightened emotional moments, the more irrational thoughts find their way to the surface and unintentionally present as insincere and aggressive. Sometimes, it's as simple as slowing down and processing the situation.

Take this example: A couple seated for dinner at a restaurant begins to argue. One partner says something hurtful to the other, and the situation escalates. This exchange continues until one says, "I hate you!" In that instant, immediate regret settles in. This is a moment when someone was not in touch with their core. The words were not a true depiction of how that partner feels on a regular basis, nor how they wanted to express their frustration.

The closest people in that person's life may know that this one moment is not who they really are. But a passerby or new acquaintance may assume that comment accurately represents that person. In reality, this couple has loved one another for decades, and one thought in a heated argument led to a completely off-base statement. Had the individual slowed down and evaluated their true feelings and the outcome they wanted, they would have settled into a truer and freer self. The next words out of their mouth would have been a better reflection of who they are and what their partner means to them.

By taking the moment to reset, the "I hate you" would never have come out. Instead, accounting for their actual span of emotions and love for their partner, that next statement would have sounded more like, "I'm frustrated with where this is going. I'm getting upset with you and how you are talking to me, and I'm upset with how I am talking to you. This is not us." That is the better representation of the person's overall self and the relationship.

Keeping in mind who you are will help when you find yourself challenged in extraordinary circumstances. Whether you find yourself in such moments frequently or rarely, you must improve at being yourself and being honest. When you feel an outburst creeping up or your anger and frustrations rising, evaluate the thought in terms of how you really feel and what you really want. Take a pause to match that with the words you use to express it.

As you understand and challenge yourself in these circumstances, it will become easier to express yourself as you truly and freely are in the moment. In future scenarios, you'll better process your mind, mouth, and emotions to align the three accordingly. That's honesty at its best.

A Note on Brutal Honesty

Before we move on to the other half of real communication, we must address the concept of brutal honesty. Simply put, brutal honesty is the wrong way to deliver honesty. We often have people ask us to be "brutally honest" with them. At first, we applauded these individuals. They were clear on what they wanted and willing to ask for it. But we soon discovered that this was not the way to deliver honesty, requested or not. You may give it that way but don't expect it to be well received. Several relationships in our lives have been damaged because of brutal honesty.

The correct way to give your honesty is to be 100 percent honest and 100 percent loving at the same time. Take *brutal* out of the equation; it doesn't belong. In fact, it's a guaranteed method to end any communication that might have been occurring. Brutal is a direct shot taken at someone's openness. The brutality serves only to shut down the other person and give us a fleeting moment of satisfaction. There is no need to rip another person down to get how you really feel across the table.

> The correct way to give your honesty is to be 100 percent honest and 100 percent loving at the same time.

Ken shares the following story:

Years ago, I had a colleague with whom I shared my brutal honesty about their work performance. My mindset was nowhere near being loving. I thought to myself, "Okay, I'm ready; here I go. I'm going to share exactly what I think and precisely how I feel. I'm coming at them with my sword." And that was my approach.

I delivered this brutal honesty, and it burned the bridge between us ever since. It was a mistake. To be brutal means *savagely violent*, and it came out exactly that way. The way I delivered honesty was inhumane and wrong. This manifestation of honesty doesn't belong in real communication. To be 100 percent honest and 100 percent loving is a difficult request. It is not easily done but completely attainable.

Ever since this screwup, I've worked hard to strengthen my loving approach. I make sure to begin a difficult topic with care. Using the Agreement (see Chapter 6) and some extra love, I tell them, "What you are asking for is for me to be 100 percent honest with you, and I will do that. But you must be 100 percent open to receiving whatever I share with you. And what I share, you must know, comes from a place of love. I care about you, so I am going to be honest with you. And then, please, let's keep the conversation going so we can unpack it and understand it together." Any difficult conversation is much better received when we begin in this manner. You will still need to deliver 100 percent honesty but adding in 100 percent loving is the better approach.

The Other Half of Real Communication

We've explored honesty, given stories, and poured ourselves out, but honesty alone is not enough to have real communication. In fact, honesty without the other half of the equation is useless. Remember, there are two key parts to real communication: openness and honesty.

> **Without openness, honesty is meaningless.**

We've started with honesty because that is arguably the sexier half of the equation. It's what we're drawn to first. Our ego loves to hear us talking about ourselves. We love the idea of "me, myself, and I," but honesty falls flat without openness. There is no place for our thoughts, feelings, or words to land without openness. Without openness, honesty is meaningless. As you work on your honesty, be sure to bring your openness right alongside it.

This next chapter is the most important part of the whole book. It is *the* game changer. It is society's missing piece. It will set you and others free: Openness.

4

Essentials of Openness: *Bringing Real Communication to Life*

H ave you ever asked someone to be "open and honest"?
What did you *really* mean by asking that?
Right now, we're approaching the concept of being "open" in an incorrect manner. In the pages to come, we will rethink openness and use it in a way that will better suit you, your relationships, your community, society, and the world. When we hear people use this phrase on shows, we find that they are often not embracing both words. At least not in the way that would be most meaningful to each of us. When stated, most people tend to give *open and honest* a singular meaning. They focus on how the phrase applies to themselves rather than all the people in the conversation. They skip the most important part of the phrase—*open*—in turn, making the word meaningless.

The problem is we can't wait to talk about ourselves and lean into the honest part of "open and honest." It's all a little silly because being honest is pointless without an open party to receive it. Some take the open part in "open and honest" to mean transparency, but if you are being honest, that's already the case. We need to focus on both being honest *and* being open.

We mentioned earlier two of the healthy rules we share with our clients when we begin our workshops: *Be* open and *be* honest. We purposely separate them. In the past, we would encourage clients to be "open and honest" as one phrase, but that wasn't nearly as effective as separating the two. When saying "be open and honest," most clients would not hear or acknowledge the open part to mean listening. Many, especially our more aggressive type A clients, couldn't wait to deliver their honesty, at times, forgetting that communication is a two-way street.

Most individuals are not ready to listen. Instead, everyone is ready to preach, instruct, or spew their viewpoint across the table. This self-serving approach desperately needs to be balanced out. When using The Pursuit of Honesty® Assessment, nearly every team has scored lower on openness compared to their honesty. We help them to embrace both sides of communication with an absolute willingness to be open to the others in the room. If eight billion people took an open stance, we would create more room for people to be heard. Instead of a singular, egotistical approach, we would acknowledge others by listening to them. The simple act of listening creates greater belonging for everyone.

In today's divisive world of constant opinion, expectations, and noise, it's becoming increasingly difficult to be open. The sheer lack of openness within people creates a wall dividing you from everyone else. That wall rises from our insecurities, past pains, fears, anxiety, and selfishness. It is being exacerbated by social media, misinformation, and a lack of real communication. To combat these various walls, we must focus on openness and put the effort into listening to others rather than embracing ourselves. As we learn to utilize both openness and honesty whenever we're in conversation, we create a foundation of strong relationships, understanding, and humanity. Openness and honesty are skills we can develop to eliminate division, exclusion, aggression, and alienation.

Clarifying the Openness Side of Communication

To make openness most effective, let's keep it simple. The definition: Openness is listening without reservation, putting your needs and wants on pause for someone else.

Like honesty, we've gone deeper and discovered the three essentials of openness. It is often the tougher hill to climb, making it crucial we keep it simple.

Without openness, honesty is meaningless.

The Three Essentials of Openness are:

1. Listen Without Reservation™
2. Taking It In and Letting It Go
3. About Others

Use the definition, three essentials, and what follows to raise your levels of openness higher. Let's unpack each essential.

The First Essential: Listen Without Reservation™

Whether we're aware of it or not, we all have a constant monologue in our minds. We take note of our surroundings, prepare a snappy comeback, and add to our to-do list. But most concerning, we often judge other people without first being open to what they are saying. We don't keep our egos in check. We don't slow it down, we don't evaluate its ramblings, and we don't even consider whether we agree with what that little voice is saying. And when it has a response ready to launch before the other person has finished speaking, we've lost our opportunity to engage in real communication.

That is why the first essential of openness is to listen without reservation. We don't give ourselves the opportunity to really hear what another person is saying. Listening to understand rather than to respond is what we are getting at. We encourage a pause between when someone ends their sentence, and someone else begins. There's no need to immediately fill the space with words. That small pause is your brain processing the full statement and giving a higher level of honesty back.

The second part is *without reservation*, and this is where the greater challenge lies. Often, we come into a conversation protecting our own point of view, as if it is the only one that matters. We frequently treat our opinions as facts or positions as if our perspective is *always* superior to anyone else's. We look at another human being, Democrat or Republican, Christian or atheist, immigrant or native, and make a snap judgment about them based on what we've been taught, believe, or experienced, rather than connecting with them, seeking to understand who they are and where they are coming from. Connection and communication are a two-way street. If we are not open to someone, we ought not expect them to be open to us or our honesty.

Ken shares the following:

> In the past, I couldn't stand it when someone made assumptions about me based on how I talked, looked, or what I believed. But I made those exact assumptions about others quite often, actually. I was

not listening without reservation. My judgmental and assumptive positions brought me no greater happiness. If anything, they brought me down and made me more aggressive and less loving toward others. I was shutting people out rather than letting them in. But throughout my work and experiences, I've come to understand my past actions, and I'm working to resolve them. Listening to others without reservation has brought me more joy, peace, understanding, and appreciation for those who cross my path.

We divide and isolate ourselves through a lack of openness in countless ways—from innocuous preferences like Coke vs. Pepsi, dogs vs. cats, or Nike vs. Adidas to more insidious issues such as war, artificial intelligence, and political ideology. No matter what side of the debate you land on, it is often difficult to be open to the other side.

A Gendered Conversation

Grace shares such an example:

"You would not believe the sexism I experienced today!" I said as I flopped down on the couch after a long day. "Oh?" is all Eric had to respond with before I launched into it.

"You know the pink bag I have, the one I use for work with my laptop and everything in it?" He nodded. "Well, I had it on as a backpack today because I was walking outside from meeting to meeting, and lugging it on one side is a pain. Anyway, at an event, I met this man, probably in his late forties or early fifties. We had a nice conversation talking about what we do for work and what was coming up in our lives. He talked about his kids a bit, and I shared about the wedding." At this point, Eric and I were about six months away from saying "I do," so it was top of mind.

"Then we get to the end, and as we're about to walk our separate ways, he says to me, 'You look like you're all ready for kids after the wedding with that bag!' and I was stunned. I couldn't believe he'd just said that to me. In what world is that normal to say? And then he just walked away."

Eric looked at me with his head cocked.

"What?" I asked.

"Are you sure he meant it to be sexist?" he questioned.

"I'm sure he didn't mean it that way, but no one would ever say anything like that to a man! When's the last time someone said anything about having kids to you?"

"Well, never, I guess, but—"

I cut him off. "Exactly. Women get it all the time, though. Just based on our biology, people assume we want or can have kids, but that's just not how it works. And it's also not okay to comment on it unsolicited!"

"Okay. But we've talked about it and are planning on having kids, so I guess I'm confused," he said.

"But he didn't know that, and for him to say so was completely unnecessary."

"Haven't you said things you regret later and wish you hadn't said?"

I huffed, "Of course, but I would never say something so sexist like that. And not one person has ever made a comment like that about my bag."

"True, but maybe to him, it looked like what he's seen other moms with, and said it without thinking. I don't think he meant to be sexist."

Annoyed at not getting the reaction I expected, I muttered, "Maybe," and we left the conversation at that. I thought he'd have the same perspective I did and jump into justified anger with me. But instead, I was left to consider the interaction differently from my initial interpretation.

A few weeks later, I ran into the same man at a networking event. After the conversation with Eric, rather than bracing myself for more sexism and holding onto my reservations, I chose to lean into more openness. Again, the time was pleasant, and he introduced me to another person by saying, "She really knows her stuff. You two should talk!" His kind endorsement took me by surprise. The preconceived notions I had based on his 'sexist comment' wouldn't equal the support he'd just given me. Again, I found myself wondering.

Toward the end of the event, we again found ourselves in the same circle of conversation. I was explaining the type of organizations we work with, highlighting that I personally love supporting businesses and nonprofits. After I finished, he said, "I'm working with a nonprofit right now actually. They have about thirty people on staff. Once we're all set with the paperwork, I'll introduce you to them."

"Wow, that'd be great. Thanks!" I said as I found myself stunned, but this time for a different reason.

Had I chosen to write off that man and no longer have any interest in what he had to say, I would have been the one to miss out, not him. If my snap judgments and reservations had won out, my life would be constantly dictated by my reactions rather than my values. I believe deeply that each human being has inherent value, whether they believe what I believe or see the world differently. My lack of openness was risking my ability to understand this man.

Sexism and gender bias are pervasive and toxic, but with closer inspection and understanding, that was simply not what was happening between the two of us. I jumped to assumptions, rather than leading with openness. -

With real communication, we engage in conversations that otherwise would never happen and leave us worse off for it. By staying in community and conversation with this man—in other words, by remaining *open*—my preconceived notions became unfounded, and a relationship was able to persist.

Consider where openness will do the same for you. It is impossible to make meaningful change and progress, especially when we impose our own desires upon everyone else. When we meet someone with openness, people can sense the potential for reciprocity. Modeling openness and honesty will increase your chances of getting it back in return. The more we rid ourselves of our divisive nature using openness the easier it is to move forward together.

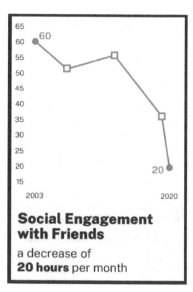

Social Engagement with Friends

a decrease of **20 hours** per month

To say that you have not lived in someone else's shoes is a giant understatement. You've lived one life; you do not have access to anyone else's. You can't possibly fully understand what led them to certain beliefs and values. The least we can do is be open to someone else's honesty. We can give them one moment where we put our needs and wants on pause. When we release the need to control or change them, we

58

are giving them peace and a space to be themselves. When you see the world through a lens of openness, your empathy and understanding grow. Rather than being a divisive member of society, you become a productive one.

Not listening to others and focusing solely on our own needs and wants results in fewer relationships and shared spaces. As of 2023, the US Surgeon General has declared loneliness the new public health epidemic, stating, "Loneliness and isolation represent profound threats to our health and well-being." From 2003 to 2020, social engagement with friends decreased from sixty hours a month to a low of twenty hours a month (see graph).[3]

In this same study, social isolation increased, and all areas of social engagement decreased, including companionship. The health impacts are as stated: "Loneliness and social isolation increase the risk for premature death by 26% and 29%, respectively." These statistics were gathered right before the global COVID-19 pandemic, which only pushed us toward further isolation. Our lack of openness and honesty have more dangerous outcomes than just being able to communicate with others. When we are without real relationships, we're literally risking our lives. Let that sink in. When we disconnect from one another, and our lives become isolated and directionless, our very existence and purpose are threatened.

We create that divide and isolation when we're unwilling to put aside the reservations and judgments we often immediately place on others, hence the emphasis on listening *without reservation*. This behavior is a hurdle to connecting with one another. For us to get the full advantages of openness, we must realize the huge barrier in front of us: a lack of connection. It is easy to coast through life and forget how important it is to connect through open and honest communication. We easily fall into an isolated life. Sometimes, we get lazy, complacent, and self-absorbed—too lazy to pick up the phone and call, too lost in our own world to spend the time with a friend, too quick to judge rather than hear someone out. We're losing the ability to care about other human beings, especially those who see the world differently than us.

After countless hours in the session room and in social circles, we've felt and seen the ability to listen decline rapidly. And not just hearing someone but going deep to actually understand. At this point, listening isn't just a God-given gift to humans; it's a skill we need to relearn and maintain.

Consider this story from Father Joshua Caswell, a Catholic priest, about an unexpected connection and subsequent relationship:

I met Brooke at a coffee shop across the street from my parish. We started off as acquaintances and eventually became really good friends. We talk a lot and sometimes go for lunch. Brooke also happens to be a leader of a feminist group, but this hasn't stopped our friendship.

I remember clearly this moment of humanity we shared when I showed up in downtown Chicago for a pro-life march. I was on a bus with more than sixty kids and adults. We pulled up on this street where the police had created a physical separation between those marching and those protesting it.

There were thousands upon thousands of people there that day in Chicago, on either side of the issue. There were signs and chants everywhere. The vitriol and hatred were palpable.

The bus pulled right in between both sides. I got off, easily identifiable as a Catholic priest in my full black robe and collar. And I suddenly saw Brooke, on the other side of the street, counter-protesting. Without a word, she began walking toward me.

We met in the middle of the road. Here we were, Brooke and me on literal opposite sides, separated by police, opinions, and even hate at times. Yet, we were still friends. We exchanged a hug right in the middle of it all. A hug witnessed by all. A hug that left everyone confused.

The moment you mention you're a priest, there's a preconceived notion about what that entails and how I'm judging someone. Certain defenses rise, and it becomes difficult to connect with the other person. But Brooke and I had moved past those defenses, seeing each other as full humans rather than a list of opinions and values we disagree on.

I've learned that the moment you recognize somebody as a human being, you know there's more to the story. I've often entered unwittingly, even without my collar, into a stanza of people's lives. I get to be a part of their story and witness the mystery that they are because I'm willing to see and love the totality of who they are. At the end of the day, I'm left feeling that I live a meaningful life, having faith in God and humanity.

To listen without reservation, we need to release control the moment someone else speaks. While someone else is sharing their thoughts, we work hard to hear and absorb what they're saying without coloring it with our thoughts, concerns, or beliefs. We must be completely present and focused on them. Brooke and Father Joshua are opposed on heavily controversial issues, and yet, their relationship persists because they've developed these skills. We need to fully embrace what is being said as it is being said. Just for a moment, we practice putting our own needs and wants on pause to listen to someone else. A masterful communicator isn't in the conversation only to serve themselves but to be present for another person.

What our society must do is reach those who would never pick up this book on their own. We must strive to create connection, to come back together again, to create community, all with the power of real communication. It must be a collective effort on our part to bring those people along with us and not leave them in isolation.

To put this essential to the test, go have a conversation. Every time your mind begins to wander or your own thoughts take over, return to listening to the other person. Whether it's a store clerk checking out your groceries, a family member you've been at odds with, or a coworker expressing a complaint, get in their shoes, listen without reservation, and understand them. You'll still have your chance to reply with honesty, but let the other person have the spotlight for a moment. Go experience just one little moment where your needs and wants aren't the only thing in the world.

> **Go have a conversation. Every time your mind begins to wander or your own thoughts take over, return to listening to the other person.**

The Second Essential: Taking It In and Letting It Go

This second essential, taking it in and letting it go, tackles releasing what someone else has shared and any negative effects it may have on us. We are often so attached to our ideals and values that anyone holding an opposing view comes across as a threat. Many times, we don't absorb what is being shared. We guard ourselves against that "threat," which cuts us off from any potential connection. When we do take it in, we struggle to let it go. It lingers, festering and slowing our ability to move through life.

In a world of eight billion people, the sheer volume of differences presents a stark reality to us. Every person is unique and different. Each human life is a miracle, a scientific improbability that came to fruition. And so here we are, tasked with navigating this gift together. In a world filled with disagreements and massive egos, it is the challenge of our lifetimes.

Disagreement becomes painful not because of opinions or statements but the noise our mind makes about those opinions and statements. Our minds generate that noise in the form of judgment, anger, expectations, assumptions, reservations, and so on. It's our egocentric and busy minds that create the friction. Instead of remaining open to the opposing side, we build walls, create division, and put space between ourselves and the person we are talking with. We create more friction about our disagreements than any of those conversations ever deserved.

We are not taking in a message because we are so busy fighting it and favoring our own understanding. We leave little room for others, rarely letting people have their moments, thoughts, or feelings. This "taking it in" is half the battle; the other half is "letting it go."

In the rare moments when we genuinely listen to someone else, we often leave what they've said trapped inside ourselves. We don't let it go, and some things ought to be let go. We dwell on the negative as opposed to the positive. Our minds hook onto a thought or idea, and we beat ourselves up, never releasing the disagreement or conflict that took place. Instead of processing the thought and letting it go, we hang on for dear life. We take in the good and bad, tending to let go of the good and hold on to the bad. What we're holding on to is holding us down.

The idea of "you are what you eat" applies here. The more you hang on to the neg-

What you're holding on to is holding you down.

ative, the more it makes up who you are. The more you hang on to the positive, the more it makes up who you are. This is a choice for us all. When we choose to let things in, we can also choose to let things go. This is not to say ignore the negative, but simply choose to let it go quickly. Take it in, acknowledge it, process it, and move on.

The road is riddled with thousands of little disagreements we can study as examples. Consider how often a bad driving experience has ruined your day. "This guy nearly ran me off the road this morning! Can you believe that?" What makes it worse is that this is often an evening conversation about a morning event. One action held a person captive in anger and disbelief for hours. It's simply a thought taking hold, ruining our opportunity to be the best version of ourselves.

Ken expands on what we've all experienced while driving:

> One summer, I was driving on some back roads, planning to take a left-hand turn. A huge shrub blocked my path to see potential oncoming traffic. With little room for viable options, I went for it. As soon as I did, I saw a truck coming and closing in fast. I got into my lane with no room for error. I just made it on time and caused some panic for the other driver. They blasted their horn, making it known that they disagreed with my actions. In days past, my thoughts would have been, "Here is a big fat middle finger for you for not understanding this turn is a tricky one."
>
> But today, I process the thought. I think of the other person more than I think of me. I understand that they can't see what I see or think about what I could have done differently, and then I let it go. I move on, and my day goes on largely unhindered. We have the choice to let it go.

Driving is a minor example of disagreement. People have years of trauma they struggle to purge. Some of our clients have shared their deepest thoughts, regrets, and buried feelings, and by doing so they've chosen to let the trauma of the past out. They are actively taking the time and exhibiting the courage to acknowledge it and let go.

When in the session room, we like to use breathing as an analogy for this essential. We're inhaling and exhaling every minute of the day. If we are not open, we aren't inhaling anything. If we are listening—taking it in but not letting it go—we are not exhaling and, therefore, suffocating. When we inhale, our body must process that air by taking what it needs, oxygen, and exhaling what it doesn't, carbon dioxide. This is the beauty of openness. We cannot control what we inhale, that is, another person's honesty, but we do have the choice of keeping what we need and exhaling the rest. We do not need to hold on to the stress and anxiety we create around unavoidable conflict and disagreement. Simply exhale it.

If previous disagreements and instances of pain are still festering inside you, know that you can still exhale those as well and practice letting it go. Not too long ago, one of our professional peers learned this firsthand.

Here's what he discovered:

Before becoming an EOS Implementer®, I had a business in the financial and lending industry for over thirty years. It is a scarcity-minded industry with little shared trust. It's like a game of musical chairs, except when the music stops, you pull out a gun, shoot the person next to you, and take their chair.

That is not how I'm naturally hardwired, and consequently, I spent thirty-three years trying not to behave that way. Building our team and a culture in that environment was difficult, but we made it work. We cared about our clients and did our best to do it all the right way. And in doing so, we carved out a niche for ourselves.

Some years into the business, we understood we needed to be acquired by a bigger firm to continue our growth. This is where we, and I specifically, missed the boat—big time. We thought it was a good fit with people who seemed to be some of the nicest in our industry. The culture felt like one built on teamwork, helpfulness, and love.

We did the deal and merged our companies. It wasn't six months into it that I found their entire culture was a façade. I came to see that they were the most scarcity-minded and worst-behaved people I had met in my entire career. The deception and underhanded actions all took place behind the scenes at the expense of their clients and employees. It was horrible. I knew I had to get myself and my people out, but they wouldn't let us simply leave; they threatened serious legal action that would ruin our lives. It took six years of careful planning, but eventually, we did get every single employee out of that business.

Some years later, I decided to become an EOS Implementer® and signed up for bootcamp. Walking into the room the first day was like an immediate flashback to the culture we had merged with, and I was absolutely triggered. I had been so excited to join the community but felt this overwhelming sense of dread and fear. Sitting there, I thought, "What the hell did I just get myself into?"

I knew I loved EOS®, but I was scared. My past experience was a hell I didn't want to live through ever again. I still harbored a lot of resentment against that business owner. So much anger remained built up inside me even three years later. We were still in the same circles publicly, and he attempted to keep up the façade of a friendship. I couldn't stand it.

I knew I had to figure out a way to let this feeling go if I wanted to continue with my business and my life. As a spiritual man, I began to say one genuine prayer for him every week. Wishing good things for him and his employees was so hard to do, but it was the best thing I could have ever done.

You see, he wasn't affected by my anger, resentment, and frustrations. I was the one being weighed down by it, getting crushed and held back from doing what I wanted. When a memory from that time would come up, my heart would start racing, and I'd get angry and anxious and lose all focus. It disrupted my life regularly.

But by working to let it go through prayer, I now feel free. The weight of those emotions is completely gone. There is no heart-racing rage when I see him at business functions around town. I'm able to embrace the EOS® community and enjoy the culture for what it truly is—loving and abundance-minded. I can live my life much easier now because I've been able to let it go.

His ability to let go and choose openness brought him calmness and peace he never would have experienced otherwise and a new community with unending opportunities. Letting go is the most difficult yet most rewarding part of practicing openness. Only you can choose to hold tightly to all the things that bother you and ignite your anger. You can determine when it's worth the stress of trying to control another person—or whether repeatedly returning to the past is helping or hurting you. While prayer was his methodology for letting go, many options are available to us. A few include journaling, therapy, meditation, or coaches. Find what works for you, take in the honesty, process it, and then let it go. Inner peace is waiting on the other side.

Peace can be a choice made by letting it go and simply letting others be truly and freely themselves. Your level of stress and discomfort affects only you. Think about what it would feel like to lift that weight off your shoulders by even just a small amount. Being open will do that for you. You'll notice greater peace as you're better able to take it in *and* let it go.

The Third Essential: About Others

Openness is about others. We cannot escape the people with whom we share this world. Believe whatever you want (we promise to be open to it), but we can't deny what we believe to be a spiritual force that has put each specific individual here at this exact time. Life and all its complexity is too improbable to be a coincidence. And if that is the case, we must decide what we are to do with our time here together.

Do we spend it only serving ourselves, without helping or building up others?

Or can we imagine a world in which we value every individual and lean into serving others as often or more than ourselves?

Openness helps us become less self-centered and puts us on a path of caring for the entire world. If we want to have our honesty and be truly and freely ourselves, we must couple it with openness and share in the experiences and perspectives of others. Being open to another human being is an act of respect and, to a certain extent, an act of love for that person. To truly be open to others, we need to recognize the value of each individual and their unique experiences and listen without reservation to them.

> Openness helps us become less self-centered and puts us on a path of caring for this world of humans collectively.

We've been blessed to serve dozens of organizations that care about their people. So much so that they designed their organizations for the greater good of their people, not always their profits. They hire us to help the organization be better to those within it—to help them do better together. The issue organizations struggle with is not how any one individual operates but how the collective does. We're all dysfunctional; we all hold on to our egos and favor our ideas, feelings, and thoughts, but we rarely come together to create something better.

Here is an example from Ken:

One such organization is Habitat for Humanity® of Kent County, Michigan. Bev Thiel, executive director, is one of my favorite leaders I've ever worked with. She took over the organization from a past, beloved executive director. She came into an environment of what we call "West Michigan Nice." Great people who didn't want to ruffle a feather. People who would be agreeable, nod, and do what is asked of them. But after they shut the doors of the meeting room, the hallways swelled with disagreements of their leadership, displeasure with the direction, and discontent with seemingly every action. The organization was suffering, there was no clear direction, and their people weren't aligned. It was an unhealthy environment.

I often imagine Bev being promised an incredible job filled with rainbows and butterflies but walking into a place spattered with various colors over the walls, furniture, and windows with butterflies trapped in the paint. It was a messy situation, and I could see the weight she carried.

During one of our first sessions together, I asked the team to evaluate one another on how they lived the core values. One of their longtime employees put up immediate resistance. I distinctly remember them saying, "How can you ask me to evaluate someone who just started, is my boss, and essentially has my job in her hands?" You don't have to read into this one too far to realize that this team was not willing to expose the true condition. I was met with resistance like I'd never seen before. Honesty to them was a threat, and the fear of retaliation was real. They all wanted to run from the shock of what they were about to endure.

The team wanted to remain stagnant and avoid change, but deep down, they knew they needed something different. They weren't open and certainly weren't listening without reservation. In fact, every time they heard a new initiative or approach, I felt the reservations and objections from their energy and body language alone. Each wanted to maintain what they had, hold on to an executive director who was no longer there, and not open themselves up.

To create change, the organization needed two things:

- to commit to improvement
- to embrace openness

For the first year together, I watched as Bev tried to outmaneuver the dysfunction to get the team on the right track. I sounded like a broken record, saying, "Trust the process" and "Listen to each other without reservation." For an organization built to be about others, it sure seemed hard to move past everyone's motives. I reached the point where I doubted my own resolve, the process, and my ability to break through. I could feel my need for control getting in the way. I was becoming less patient, less willing to listen, and wanting to plow through the issues. I began to model a lack of openness, rendering me counterproductive. I was becoming the enemy of their progress.

Something had to change for the team, and it started with me. I decided to slow down the process after much reflection on my aggressiveness, blaming, and impatience. I increased the number of calls with Bev and focused hard on just listening. During sessions, I became more open to their complaints and frustrations with their organization. I saw their biggest resistor open up and give more to the team. And then Bev did the same. I asked the team more questions about how they felt, what frustrated them, and what they needed for their organization. It became less about me, Ken, and what I wanted the team to do. It became more about others.

Two things came from practicing and modeling openness with that team. First, the picture of their true condition became clearer for me because I allowed them to help paint it instead of imposing my will. Second, their trust was being built. Instead of bulldozing one another or choosing passive aggressiveness, the team created more space for everyone to be heard and understood. That kind of openness creates an incredible opportunity to increase trust. And it did just that.

The team went from being closed off to a much more open organization. They've moved from stagnant and frustrated to expediting ideas and executing them faster, experiencing a higher level of trust, and enjoying a healthy leadership team. It has been an incredible learning opportunity for us and built a lasting friendship between my client and me.

Making communication about others allows us to step outside ourselves and invite those around us into a deeper conversation. We're able to see them for who they are rather than how they might serve us. Working in teams, being part of a family, and enjoying any relationship means we must be open to the collective. Being open to those around us is how we best serve one another. By setting our ego aside, we're really putting others first, letting them take the stage. Openness is about others.

Openness is the greatest gift we could ever give to another person. It is what makes honesty possible, allowing others to be truly and freely themselves. The three essentials of openness are what will set us free.

1. Listen Without Reservation™
2. Taking It In and Letting It Go
3. About Others

Our ability to be open will solve our disconnection and create more peace around the world. Strengthen your skill of openness and watch as the world transforms when you're listening without reservation, putting your needs and wants on pause for someone else.

Meet Resistance with Curiosity

Anytime we find ourselves experiencing resistance, whether toward another person, idea, or project, we have temporarily lost the ability to be open. Resistance is a wall that breaks down any potential for connection. We may experience resistance as rejection, anger, frustration, defiance, or disgust. At that point, we can no longer effectively create real communication, and we begin to isolate ourselves again.

But we have a different option available to us. When that resistance starts to rise, rather than assume negative intent, we can meet resistance with curiosity. We begin by being internally curious, asking ourselves questions such as:

Why am I resisting this person or their idea?

What happens if I continue to resist rather than be open?

Do I understand enough of what's going on, or do I need more information?

And so on. In this way, we quickly return to openness rather than letting the resistance win out. Then, because openness is *about others*, we must turn our curiosity toward that person and choose to engage with them. We experience this often with new clients who are just beginning to understand openness and honesty, misusing the definitions, or don't seem to get it. The temptation to resist and become frustrated with them is high, especially if we've just covered everything in-depth. Instead, we use curiosity to understand where they're at, using phrases such as:

What makes you feel that?

Am I experiencing resistance from you on this topic? (if yes) Can you clue me in as to why?

Can you share with me what you are thinking?

We also encourage everyone to push back on us and question the philosophy we share, therefore encouraging them to engage in curiosity

When you meet resistance with curiosity, you quickly return to openness.

rather than resistance. In doing so, we're inviting ourselves and them into deeper communication and helping us better understand each other. When you meet resistance with curiosity, you quickly return to openness.

Interrupting Is Not Openness

There are times in conversations when one person is taking up more than half of the exchange, and the urge to interrupt bubbles over, and we cut in. In that moment, our openness nosedives. The need to speak indicates we've stopped listening without reservation and cut off their honesty. We are no longer seeking to understand but rather only want to make our voices heard. It's clear to the person on the other side that we're no longer interested in connecting with them.

Take the presidential debates as an example of this. As two people debate, they model for the world that there is not a togetherness. There is only winning or defeating the other person. The two will constantly talk over one another, exhibiting a complete lack of openness.

This jump to interrupt also happens in group conversations when we fear our voice won't be heard. We might interrupt another person mid-sentence, whether out of excitement for what they're saying or because we can no longer hold back what we have to say. Rather than waiting our turn, we become irresponsible with our honesty and miss the opportunity to hear and help others share. As we become masterful communicators, our need to interrupt lessens, and we're better able to help each person in the conversation have their moment too.

Grace recalls working with a client who helped illuminate the need for more openness in group settings:

During the workshop, I asked the group to think about times they lacked honesty and why that happened. Rob, a quiet and thoughtful man, pondered it for a moment and said, "For me, it happens when I'm in a group. People are usually talking so fast that I don't have the time to process, and no one seems to notice if I'm silent the whole time." He explained that there's not a pause for him to be able to speak in the conversation, and so he tended to avoid such interactions. Rob is a brilliant communicator and can summarize a topic or conversation in a succinct and profound manner. I knew people were missing out on brilliance because they were unable to use openness to create a space for Rob.

When we're intentional about creating real communication and open and honest environments, we notice people like Rob: those who've yet to have the opportunity to share because someone is either controlling the entire conversation or no one has invited them to participate. We then have the choice to create openness for them and their honesty to create another level of connection.

When we encounter others who dominate conversations or find ourselves doing so, we also find a lack of openness. If there is not an even exchange because one person hijacks the whole conversation, we have an absence of real communication. We must be willing to give the other person the space for their honesty using our skill of openness and trust that our opportunity will come. Now, if that doesn't happen, we must forsake our openness for a moment and invite that person into a more real exchange. In Chapter 6, you'll learn how to do this effectively using The Agreement. Openness is a skill for you to deploy.

Being open to another person's honesty does not mean we have to agree with them. In fact, it makes for better connection and conversation when we disagree with love and respect. This serves as a reminder to be 100 percent honest *and* 100 percent loving. Being open does not require us to condone their thoughts and values or support what they're saying. Openness is simply allowing someone else to have the space to be heard. It is possible to have differing opinions and still listen to each other. No progress can be made when either party is unable to hear each other. It's not about winning or controlling; it's about being and allowing others to be.

Openness gives everyone's honesty meaning. That is the essential point here: Open + Honest = Real Communication. By being both open and honest, every relationship has the chance to be real. To be meaningful. To be authentic. With "me, myself, and I" not being the focal point in everything we do, we have more opportunities to truly connect with those around us. Simply put, being open is one of the greatest gifts you can give to all the human beings around you. If you were to take nothing else away from our work together other than understanding and practicing openness, you would have accomplished a great deal and be better for it. Thus far, we've presented many lessons and examples to you, but this one is unequivocally the most important. It enhances our relationships, mental health, and lives.

Now, we'll put the two together and understand how real communication transforms ourselves, others, and our relationships.

5

Real Communication Is...
Open + Honest

Open + Honest = Real Communication

et's start with a basic definition that will carry us through this conversation. At its core, real communication is *when two parties engaged in a conversation or exchange are both open and honest.* Our honesty kicks off the exchange of real communication. It all starts with sharing an honest thought, opinion, perspective, feeling, or idea. On the other side, the person or party is listening to that honesty without reservation, allowing a moment to take in the information, and in return, giving back their honesty. To the degree that each party maintains their skills of being open and honest equals their ability to receive and deliver real communication. Ideally, this cycle persists for the duration of the conversation, resulting in high levels of real communication.

Ken relates this personal experience:

There was a point in my life when real communication was nowhere to be found and it put my marriage at risk. I'll never forget the dagger of words Ilse, my wife, shared with me at the end of one of our long, silent fights—words that seemed to cut through my entire body. It was the type of deep wound that can cause a relationship to falter and never recover.

Just before we had children, my wife and I got into a heated disagreement. It escalated to the point where neither of us spoke to each other. This silent fight persisted for nearly three days. What was worse, two of these days fell on a weekend when we were both home and neither had plans to leave the house to get some relief from the discomfort. We navigated our shared home and lives, having so much to say to one another but so stubborn and upset that we refused to say it.

This was the nastiest fight we'd ever had in our four years together. There was no physical altercation or verbal abuse, yet it was more brutal than any beating. The non-verbal assault we aimed at each other made the air thick and the tension palpable. It was hard to enjoy any moment when I knew Ilse was walking around the house with something to say but never saying it. And I was doing the exact same to her.

The silence felt heavy when we had to pass each other as if it was harder to walk with such a weight on our shoulders. There was occasional but brief eye contact with one another. When our eyes did meet, it felt almost accidental, trying to look away or avoid the moment where our brains processed the image of the other.

The silence allowed terrible thoughts to plague my mind. "Will she speak to me again? If she does, are we done? Will this work out? This isn't what I signed up for." A once blissful marriage rested gingerly on a cliff due to the senseless absence of communication.

It was the end of day three before we broke the silence. I remember Ilse coming down the stairs. I was in for it now. There was no option for retreat, as I was positioned on the couch and couldn't run or hide. Despite my desire to avoid engagement, we were about to face this issue head-on. She made it halfway down the stairs, stopped, and I prepared to dodge a ten-word dagger in my direction.

With courage on her face and tears in her eyes, she said, "You can fix leadership teams, but you can't fix us!"

She landed a direct hit. I sat frozen in my seat, still not willing to budge but processing what she had just said to me. A flurry of emotions came rushing in. I felt disappointed as I pondered the idea that I couldn't lead our relationship as I hoped to, defensive about my work life, and now, both jealous and sad that she had the courage to break the silence and I didn't. And from Ilse's bold statement and her pent-up emotions came her truest form of honesty. I realized that she said exactly how she felt. What I viewed as a dagger to my stubborn attitude was Ilse throwing me a life raft. I didn't hesitate to latch on to it. Two distinct and important moments took place at once: she threw a lifeline, her honesty, and I grabbed ahold of it, my openness. Finally, we had both made decisions that gave us the opportunity to connect.

She was right. I would put all my efforts into my work of fixing leadership teams. I'd frequently come home exhausted after doing everything I could to bleed like the actual owner of a business. There'd be nothing left in my tank for us by the end of the day. I couldn't "fix us" because I was choosing not to do so. I'd pick everything else but us. At that defining moment in time, Ilse saved us. She snapped me into our true condition. From that instance, I knew we had some work to do.

We sat down to discuss our situation. Before moving into the tough part of the conversation, we made an agreement. She was to be honest with me, stating precisely how she felt and being direct about what she wanted. I was to be open with her, listening without reservation and putting my needs and wants on pause as she spoke. And then vice versa—I was to respond honestly, and she was to be open.

That jump-started our conversation as we immediately began with real communication. We got down to the root of our most difficult problems. The issues weren't surface-level arguments over chore disputes or financial issues but around how we weren't communicating effectively with one another. Again, without mincing her words, Ilse told me my tone toward her felt condescending. She said it was as if I wouldn't even engage with her. When I did speak, she said I was cold, like I wasn't being my normal, loving self. I felt my defenses rise, like a wall going up, with an unthoughtful, patronizing response ready to launch.

Luckily, before I opened my mouth, I caught my flaw and recognized how counterproductive it would be. In fact, it would go to prove her exact point. I took a deep breath and refocused. An important moment of awareness came over me, helping me realize I needed to change my habitual approach. From there I made the conscious decision to focus on her, shutting down my self-serving thoughts and needs, and listen to what she had to say. Every single word of it. I did everything I could to remain open to her. And I began to understand Ilse and her perspective. I was relieved to learn more about one of the real blocks between us. Even more inspiring, I knew I had the strength to break it down. I told her I better understood her position and that I was committed to working on it.

Then came my turn. I told her it seemed my smallest requests made her defensive and upset with me. Because of this, I often couldn't talk to her or enjoy engaging in conversation. Naturally, Ilse became defensive. Her walls went up, and her ability to listen without reservation dropped. I reminded her, "We agreed to be open and honest." I continued explaining how it was hard to say anything to her, as it most often would be received defensively with anger. She began to understand the complexity we added to all our communication.

If I was regularly condescending, cold, and not expressing myself clearly to her, and she was defensive and not receptive, our communication didn't have a chance to genuinely reach one another. This conversation persisted for nearly two hours. In our discussion, I realized the pain of expecting Ilse to do exactly what I told her to do all the time. I believed I knew best and that my way was always right. But I wasn't sharing the space; I wasn't open to the other person in the room and the gifts she brought to the table. She brought a perspective I didn't have, and trying to force her into my way was only causing fights and distance between us. I was constantly attempting to design a world for just myself, not for us. We ended our conversation with a mutual commitment to do better together, to fight through the discomfort, and to iron out our communication should this arise again.

Had Ilse and I started off knowing what it meant to be open and honest, our silent fight never would have occurred. Our communication today exists on a higher level. There is less room for doubt, anxiety, animosity, and misunderstanding between us. We're clear on our commitment to each other and our children. We better articulate our wants and needs. We still have plenty to work on, but I know we can handle anything because of real communication. To this day, we look back on this time in our lives, sometimes for a laugh at how ridiculous we were and other times as a reminder that we need to be open and honest, especially when we are struggling the most.

Real communication requires two or more people to be open and honest. Knowing that 100 percent open and honest is unattainable all the time, it is the pursuit that matters the most—that two people commit to a purer, more real exchange, putting the effort into being themselves and being open to the other person. The hard truth is that we can do so much better than we are doing today. The smallest of strides in being more open and honest in all our relationships will feel like progress made in leaps and bounds.

It all begins with us. When we have the courage to share, modeling an ability to be truly and freely ourselves, we create the space for another person to share their honesty. In turn, when we model listening without reservation, we create a space that feels safe, helping someone else to feel more comfortable sharing their honesty. Exhibiting openness helps the other person to also be more open as they have an example to follow. Practicing this more regularly, speaking honestly and listening openly, will pave the way for everyone else to do so too.

The concept is a simple one to understand, but that does not mean it's easy to implement. Real communication requires us to be present, intentional, and focused, especially when first committing to it. We must clear away all the common distractions we experience, whether that comes in the form of a cell phone, email, or random thoughts unrelated to the actual conversation taking place. Not all our communication will be real communication, but we must do our best to create and experience more moments of it daily. The level of clarity, direction, and freedom found within real communication is precisely what this world needs, but it is largely absent from our day-to-day communication. The good news is anyone has the power to bring it about in any given moment.

Imagine you gathered up all the people in your life—friends, family, coworkers—and put them in a room without you where the topic was *you*. The comments made would be more truthful than what has ever been said to your face. We desire this knowledge; we want to know where we really stand with people or how they really feel about us. Imagine what you could do with that information had it been shared with you instead. Your conversations would be more real, the true condition would be on the table, and your knowledge of your relationship with someone else would be well-informed. You could make progress together instead of remaining at the surface level. All the good, bad, and ugly are valuable so long as you handle someone else's honesty with openness.

> The level of clarity, direction, and freedom found within real communication is precisely what this world needs, but it is largely absent from our day-to-day communication.

When someone offers you 100 percent honesty because they're confident you'll be 100 percent open, there is no guessing whether hidden meanings or agendas lurk in what they have to say. You will have a clear understanding of the situation –the true condition, which allows you to make the best, most informed decisions in an efficient manner. It becomes easier to solve complicated issues when no one skirts the truth to make themselves look better or holds back an opinion for fear of what the other person might think. This is where openness comes into play. When we are mutually reassured that everyone will listen without reservation and be 100 percent open, it immediately becomes easier to share. We can move through life with more freedom and a better understanding of each other.

Who Does Honesty Serve?

Quite often, it is easier to choose dishonesty or give a rose-colored version of an issue. We fear that what we have to say will hurt others' feelings and permanently damage the relationship. Instead, we say nothing or try to be nice, ultimately giving so little honesty that we might as well have said nothing. Ask yourself this:

Who does that serve?

When you are unwilling to be honest, who truly benefits from that?

Consider the feedback and perspective that an individual misses out on because we won't step into a potentially uncomfortable conversation. Their growth is hidden within the honesty that only you can give.

Grace shares this example:

As a part of concluding my workshops, I ask my teams to rate our time together on a scale of 1 to 10. I thought this particular session had gone well but knew it could have been better as it was one of my first.

As we went around the table with each team member sharing their feedback, ah-has, and rating, they all gave it a 10. While I was pleasantly surprised, confusion was setting in too. I knew I hadn't perfected my approach yet and didn't properly prepare the team for the work. I was concerned this may have been a generous "avoid conflict" type of rating. I had full faith in our content, and the team had deep conversations during our time together, but I felt that my delivery and facilitation skills still needed honing. Reflecting on the workshop afterward, I realized I had asked the team to "rate our time together," but I had taken the scoring to mean "rate my skills in leading us." Those were two different questions, and to get an answer to the latter, I turned to the team leader.

I asked her what I did well and where I needed to improve. She gave her feedback graciously and didn't hold back, just as I'd hoped. The team enjoyed the content and discussion and had great takeaways, but there was something more. Here is what she shared:

- For my facilitation, she mentioned that we spent a lot of time on the definitions of openness and honesty, where she felt the team would have been better served with more time for conversation and practicing the skills.

- The team had also previously worked with Ken, and she noticed that I followed his facilitation style closely; she encouraged me to bring more of myself into the room.

- She recommended I wear a jacket or blazer when meeting with decision-makers to exude more confidence and professionalism.

- Lastly, I often said the word "Right?" throughout our time together. This wasn't necessary and was likely a nervous habit.

This came through via email, and I read it over and over to fully understand. It was exactly what I needed to improve and continue doing the work. She mastered the balance of 100 percent honest and 100 percent loving, asking that I be open to her feedback. Her delivery ensured I could remain as open as possible to it and use it as a catalyst for growth.

Considering the first point, I adjusted my workshop timing. It helped the lesson sink in that each team I worked with would be unique, and I'd need to watch for cues on where to move faster or slower.

At this point, I'd been observing Ken facilitate for years and held his skills in high regard. I watched as he helped teams navigate difficult conversations and came out smiling afterward. I considered his way to be the best and wanted to emulate it, but I hadn't stopped to think about what my own approach would look like. I hadn't been able to see that in my attempts to emulate Ken, I neglected the unique skills I brought into the room. Her viewpoint helped me delve further into being truly and freely myself: a true gift of freedom.

Within the email, she noted that the idea of a blazer as part of an outfit was becoming more of "an old school thought," but she continued to mentor others to dress for the job they wanted. I understood her explanation and considered how it applied to me. I had tried the route of blazers but never felt fully comfortable in them. I'd find myself more distracted by it and less focused on the task at hand. I had been following the advice to dress with confidence and wear clothing that wouldn't divert my attention. Given that, I decided to continue with my blazerless style but upped my game in other areas.

Her last comment seemed small on the surface, but as I relived the workshop in my mind, I could hear myself repeatedly saying, "Right?" This was an indicator from myself that I was missing the mark. I could sense the team wasn't engaged, and instead of moving faster or pivoting to a different exercise, I vied for their buy-in by trying to elicit head nods and yeses. That warning light followed me into my following facilitations and conversations, making it clear when I needed to change directions.

Though we had spent a day together working on openness and honesty, this leader could have still chosen the easier route and glazed over my faults as a way of staying in a more comfortable conversation. She could have given me platitudes and empty praises. I would have felt her sense of hesitation with no real explanation. Instead, she chose honesty, trusting that we'd created a strong foundation built on real communication. Giving her honesty freely, confident that I would be open to it. In doing so, she illuminated gaps in my skills that otherwise would have gone unfixed, impacting my career for years to come. For this, I am forever grateful.

The next time you deliver feedback, consider for just a moment whether you're doing so with the level of honesty and love that will truly help the individual. Veiled compliments and niceties will not serve as growth opportunities. Instead, create a conversation where real communication is possible and watch them bloom.

Real Relationships

On its own, real communication intrigues people from an educational standpoint, but it becomes transformational when we apply it to our work and personal lives. Using it in this manner leads to a greater understanding of the relationships in your life. Some relationships are authentic, and some are fake. Real relationships *are those that seek out and thrive on real communication.* If we work on applying real communication in our relationships, we uncover where people really stand and how deep they are willing to go with us. You learn who is willing to commit to a more real relationship.

Real relationships *are those that seek out and thrive on real communication.*

Within our personal lives, the value of real relationships is clear. We need people who are willing to let us be truly and freely ourselves because we allow them that same freedom. We create deep bonds of love and connection. However, when it comes to the workplace, at first, it seems that value doesn't translate. We've been told work is where we stay at a surface level because we don't trust in the safety of the place. We're unsure who's willing to be open to our honesty, and, therefore, we are unwilling to be open to anyone else's. The lack of real communication is rampant.

But when we create real relationships at work, our organizations move faster. When we take the time to create trust with one another using our skills of openness, honesty, and real communication, we build an unshakeable foundation that will better withstand the tests of stress and chaos we will inevitably encounter. Real relationships at work are a requirement for those wanting to achieve more.

Ken shares the following interaction:

One of my clients, Jeff Cousins, is one of the most bold, brazen, and aggressively ambitious visionaries you could ever meet. Picture a tall linebacker, shaved head, Midwestern mob boss style. Over the years of working with this team, Jeff found himself in a significant transition, facing the first steps of giving up total control and handing his business - Kraft Business

Systems, his "baby," over to the next generation. His son, Brandon, was prepared to take over and lead the organization.

This transition was especially challenging for Jeff as he was beginning to confront the end of a beloved chapter in his life. After 30 years of owning the business and 37 years in the industry, Jeff was always willing to offer advice, direction, and decisions at a moment's notice. However, this approach sometimes limited the team's openness and honesty. His speaking time often surpassed the combined contributions of the other leaders in the room, and his reluctance to fully embrace the team's ideas left them feeling powerless. Despite numerous discussions to address this issue, Jeff's strong will and dominance consistently overshadowed our time together, resulting in a situation where Jeff "won," but the team did not.

After three years of working with the team, a pivotal moment of real communication occurred, setting Jeff and the team on a new path. Many found Jeff's dominance challenging as they tried to grow, support, and drive the business forward. Employees were incredibly loyal to him, driven by their deep commitment to the company and the family nature he had created, but for this to work, something had to change. In my work with Jeff, I focused on listening, understanding, and withholding judgment, determined to help him and the team succeed.

In one particularly intense session, Jeff's dominance reached new heights, stifling everyone else's attempts to contribute. It was too much. I intervened, asking, "Jeff, what's going on? Why do you feel the need to dominate every conversation?" He defended his position, citing his experience and industry knowledge, but continued his overpowering approach.

Sensing something deeper, I pressed further, "This isn't going to work. You committed to releasing control and supporting your team, yet here we are. What's really going on?"

In an unexpected moment of vulnerability, Jeff began to speak. "I don't know how many years I have left." This revelation was a turning point. Jeff shared about a life-threatening aneurysm he had experienced years earlier, his awareness of aging, and his anxiety about eventually passing on his beloved business. He feared letting go, concerned that Brandon and the team wouldn't be able to handle things without his guidance. "I just want them to succeed," he admitted, his eyes welling up with emotion.

This raw honesty allowed the team to see beyond Jeff's controlling persona and recognize the human being underneath. I asked Brandon to look at his father, witnessing the deep emotion pouring out. The weight of the moment spread across the team, lifting from Jeff's shoulders. His willingness to be honest created a new balance, fostering a deeper understanding among the team members. For the first time, Jeff created a safe space for dialogue, encouraging the team to share their concerns, fears, and true feelings. This moment of real communication marked the beginning of a transformation. The session evolved from the "Jeff Show" to the "Team Show," where everyone felt they belonged, connected by this shared human experience, and began to form real relationships.

Today, Jeff is not even part of the weekly, quarterly, and annual meetings. Brandon and Pat have their own leadership team that meets. Jeff receives his weekly metrics, meets with Brandon and Pat every other week, and sets the company vision, goals, and expectations. Kraft is now on the verge of surpassing its big audacious goal in almost half the expected time. Everyone is excited to see how this journey continues.

Real relationships foster belonging. Connections in your life will feel seen and heard and know they are welcome and encouraged to exchange real communication with you. That belonging the team experienced is one of our core human needs, stemming from ancient tribal days when belonging to a group of people meant the difference between life and death. Your level of belonging to the group increases your chances of survival. Although survival looks different in today's world, it is no less essential that we need to belong to survive. And in pockets of this world, survival is far less physical and far more mental.

According to a study titled "Loneliness and Social Isolation as Risk Factors for Mortality" completed by the Department of Psychology at Brigham Young University, "Actual and perceived social isolation are both associated with increased risk for early mortality." We risk an early death when we do not have real relationships in which we feel we belong.

When it comes to work, the need to foster belonging is clear. *Harvard Business Review* gives us some staggering statistics to consider. The report states that high belonging led to:

- 56% increase in job performance
- 50% drop in turnover risk
- 75% reduction in sick days
- Employees showing a 167% increase in their employer promoter score (their willingness to recommend their company to others)
- Employees receiving double the raises
- Employees securing 18 times more promotions[4]

Such results are achieved through real relationships, fostered and nurtured with real communication created by openness and honesty. We must continually invite people to share their honesty, reassuring them that we'll do our best to remain open and listen to them without reservation. When we do this, we signal to the other person that we see and value their perspective and humanity.

By unlocking the space for mutual honesty, we access the true condition of the moment. A real relationship requires that both people bring their openness and honesty to the table. It is a two-way street all the way. This isn't the space to posture or shirk your honest self. This isn't the place to disregard the lives around you. This is the space to create freedom for you and those you interact with. This is what real, meaningful human connection is all about.

> **This isn't the place to disregard the lives around you. This is the space to create freedom for you and those you interact with. This is what real, meaningful human connection is all about.**

Perhaps looking at the opposite of real relationships paints a clearer picture. What if it was all fake and every relationship you participated in was nothing more than a façade and a forgery? You are fake. They are fake. You can't trust a single word out of anyone's mouth, and you'd never dare to say exactly what you're thinking and feeling for the real fear of retribution. The true condition is nowhere in sight, and you must watch your back at every turn because there is no stable ground. Everything seems purposeless, and progress is nearly impossible. Each step you take is directionless, like navigating through a heavy fog.

The scary part is not in imagining such a world but in realizing that most of us live this way right now. The sheer lack of clarity breeds ambiguity in our lives. Uncertainty swells and, as a result, anxiety grows. This feeling can cause discomfort in our own skin because, at a primal level, we can sense nearly everyone projecting a false reality, including ourselves.

Today's most obvious example is social media. We love to share the highlights of our lives, often misrepresenting our reality and rarely showing the worst of our days. Celebrating the wins is not the issue; rather, our unwillingness to allow people into our struggles is what casts a deceptive reality. Because social media is interwoven into nearly every person's life on this planet, we are inundated with a twisted view of what life really is.

If we are to commit to real communication, we must share the lows and the highs. At the same time, if people do share their honesty, it benefits the greater population to be open to all of it. Given that most of the world is not committed to real communication (yet!), we must begin with connections that matter most, right in our own backyards and communities. Connecting with someone on LinkedIn or commenting on a Facebook birthday post is not how to foster real relationships. Oftentimes, we settle for an inauthentic level of connection because it seems easier or it's all we believe we deserve in this life. We're here to assure you that this does not need to be the case. It's time to choose real. Reflect on your current relationships

Which ones have real communication?

Which ones stay surface-level or are completely fake?

In each relationship, are you truly and freely yourself? Why or why not?

In each relationship, are you doing your part? Are you really listening without reservation? Why or why not?

Consider if you are content with each of these relationships or if you desire a deeper connection. For those relationships in which you seek a deeper connection, start by engaging in real communication. Encourage it, exhibit it, and watch the relationship transform.

An important note: Real relationships require both parties to be committed to being open and honest with each other as frequently as possible. This will require some work on your part by inviting the other party into real communication. We'll cover how to do this in Chapter 6. Have a conversation with that person and use your openness and honesty. Model the behavior by showing a little vulnerability with a personal or work-life challenge you've had. Or share this book with them and ask them what they think about real communication.

Families and the Struggles of Openness and Honesty

You may find your mind drifting toward your family when it comes to a lack of real communication. Working with organizations and teams on openness and honesty is invariably easier than doing so within families and long-lasting relationships. From the time we are born, we have relationships thrust upon us. As young children, we have very little say in who surrounds us, and we often rely on those same people for our survival. We learn to adjust our behaviors and emotions to be as appealing as possible so we can remain in the community, no matter the level of toxicity. The longer a relationship has been allowed to exist in a state of fakeness, the more work is required to direct it toward real communication. But a transformation is possible nonetheless.

Moving into adulthood, we gain independence and yet still maintain a good deal of those relationships, whether they be with family or friends. Any growth or change on our part is difficult for the community to deal with because it presents a disruption to the regular cadence. This is why bringing about more openness and honesty in those spaces is so difficult and feels impossible to some.

We hear about the aunt or uncle at the family gathering with strong political opinions, the friend who loves to tell everyone that embarrassing, old, irrelevant story about you, and the strained relationships with either their father or mother. People cannot fathom that those individuals will ever change and have resigned themselves to a subpar relationship for the rest of their lives.

Take Grace's story about her mother, for example:

My mother, Mary, is immensely proud of each of her children. She is willing to inconvenience herself if it means helping one of us, and with eight children, this is no small feat. As I've grown, my own independence has widened the gap between us and lessened the immediate needs of survival from her. Our relationship was becoming shallow, with less room for real conversations as two adults. She described herself as "not a touchy, feely person," so doing my best to respect that, I kept discussions at a surface level.

In writing this book and working with clients, the missing depth in our relationship grew louder and louder to me. How could I teach and encourage others to be open and honest while not addressing it within my own life? The hypocrisy did not sit well with me. It was time to make a change.

After completing my introduction "why" story, I asked if she would meet with me and read it. I didn't give her much context beyond it being part of the book, and that I would like her perspective. I got to the breakfast restaurant before her, ordered coffee, and sat waiting nervously. I knew what I was about to do had the potential to go sideways and leave me crushed, but I couldn't let our relationship go on as it was, either. She arrived soon after, and we started with the normal pleasantries.

I talked a bit about work, shared the latest updates, and asked if she understood what it was that Ken and I do in our business. She said she did to some degree, but not fully. As I pulled the story out of my bag, I explained to her our mission of changing how the world communicates and the definitions of openness and honesty. She nodded throughout, and before I handed over the story, I utilized the Agreement (found in Chapter 6). I remember my voice shaking, knowing that what I was asking was a hard right turn from how our communication had been. Thankfully, she agreed and began to read.

After she finished, our conversation became one that we had never had before. We talked about our experiences, and she shared more freely with me than I had expected. The hope within me was growing as I soaked in that moment. She asked for my advice on other conversations and relationships. I gave my perspective on our current communication within the family and how I could see us improving upon it.

What I once thought was impossible and was told to "simply accept and not expect it to change" transformed before my eyes. It took a bit of courage, a bundle of nerves, and the knowledge you're learning to change the course of our relationship. Is it harder when you've known the person your entire life rather than only a few weeks, such as a new colleague at work? Absolutely, it is, but it is worth that much more too. Do not remain a victim of a poor relationship simply because of its historical past. If it's one that will persist to your last days, make it a real one. Fill it with connection rather than obligation. Both of you deserve that kind of relationship.

By inviting open and honest communication, you'll gain a deeper appreciation for that person because they are being both more open and honest to whatever you have to say. The real exchanges you have in those relationships will reap massive, scalable benefits. They help the relationship gain clarity, confidence, and freedom. The more relationships surrounding you that exist in this real way, the more opportunity, meaning, and happiness you'll experience in your life.

This extends beyond family, too, into other long-standing relationships in our lives. It is a blessing to begin a new relationship with openness and honesty. There are no bad habits to break, lies to undo, or fakeness to disassemble. We can bring our whole selves as we truly and freely are. We have more control over how we choose to engage in these new experiences and relationships.

The challenge arises when your relationships don't have the chance to begin that way. We often maintain the relationship as is, not encouraging any evolution from its status quo or broken past. As we grow, progress, and shed the old versions of ourselves, not everyone will recognize those changes. The differences in our evolving selves will be subtle, like a haircut, or extreme, such as the loss of a loved one. These changes inform how we experience the world and our honesty. This, at times, can leave long-standing relationships outdated, not progressing, and growing in misunderstanding.

This work is intentionally designed to be simple, but it is not always easy. As you commit to your pursuit of honesty, the lack of real communication will become much clearer to you. If your long-standing relationship is not up to speed, it can create unexpected strain. As the relationship continues to protect the old way of interacting and communicating, the freedom of openness and honesty becomes more difficult to attain. Because most of these relationships are based on

> **As the relationship continues to protect the old way of interacting and communicating, the freedom of openness and honesty becomes more difficult to attain.**

family ties or began in childhood, much of our identity and self-understanding is wrapped up in them.

Joe Novaco, a trusted colleague, recognized this clear change with some of his older friendships:

> What energizes me the most is genuinely connecting with others. Through high school and college, I made quite a few friends. I knew the old adage that those friendships wouldn't last forever, but I hoped that wouldn't be the case for me. I'm now several years removed from those times in my life and have maintained some of those same friends, but others I've had to let go of.
>
> I was online playing some games when a notification popped up saying one of my closest friends from high school, whom I had not talked with in years, was active too. I jumped into his chat and found it filled with more of our old friends. Immediately I was reminded of the times we spent together and why I had distanced myself from these friendships. It was the most uncomfortable twenty-five minutes of my life.
>
> Nobody was being real on that call. The conversation was filled with little digs at each other. They were meant to be funny, but I could feel a hint of truth too. It was just shallow enough to shake off and yet still sting. I had joined because I wanted to hear about my friends' lives, but instead, I witnessed a complete miss on connection.
>
> At one point, I asked the group, "Are we going to talk, really? Because I'd like to. That's why I'm here. It would be really nice to hear about how you guys are doing." And then there was silence. Not one person responded. Then, someone made an unrelated, random joke, and everyone ignored what I said. I chose

to leave shortly after that and still haven't gotten a real answer from any of them.

It shocked me to see the stark difference between these old friendships and the people I surround myself with now. I felt so disappointed in the lack of connection available with those who have known me for so long. We hadn't used that length of time to mature our relationships and get to know each other more. We remained stuck at such a shallow level that I'm no longer interested in maintaining those relationships.

It's clear to me now that my relationships are building toward better and deeper bonds. The people who have stayed in my life for the long term are those who are willing to be honest with me and have real conversations. Whether we just saw each other yesterday or five years ago, there's no divide or posturing between us. I leave conversations feeling energized and known. My friends know who I truly am and continuously help me grow.

The ability to make space for openness and honesty in family and long-standing relationships requires more understanding, more education, and more communication if we want them to evolve. We're not suggesting a knee-jerk reaction but rather a step-by-step approach. We want to work at the relationship with a chisel, not a bulldozer. Any attempt to shift it suddenly will only crack the foundation of the relationship. Instead, we must commit to breaking it down piece by piece together, to replace it with a real relationship. There will be times when you falter. Your honesty will drop. Openness will disappear. This is expected. At times, you'll find yourself being fake, experiencing that very real discomfort and your newfound awareness will remind you of what real communication means for you and others. The goal is to make the relationship stronger.

Invite the people in your life to start their pursuit of honesty. Together, you'll get to explore what it means to have fulfilling and real relationships. The belonging you'll create will serve as a catalyst for your other relationships.

Know that not everyone will be willing to do this with you. When that is the case, you have a decision to make: remain and make peace with the relationship as it is, fight for it, or distance yourself from it in a 100 percent honest and 100 percent loving manner. With time and reflection, you'll know the right choice for you.

The Interconnected and Shared World

When we ask for and bring forth more moments of real communication, we are changing this world for the better. You are helping people access the true condition, deepen their real relationships, and experience the freedom of being truly and freely themselves.

We often imagine what our world would look like if we could bring real communication into some of the most controversial topics in the world: racial inequity, politics, sex, money, and morality. Today, we are living in one of the most divisive times in the United States. The mere mention of a political figure's name evokes eye rolls, cheers, or rage. We jump at the opportunity to cut down someone's argument or celebrate scandals that break down trust in the ways we run our country. It does not serve anyone to refuse to embrace real communication.

We will have the opportunity to do better together when real communication penetrates society at a greater rate than the disconnectedness. We can resolve disagreements quicker and attain clarity faster. The sheer idea that people can be more open to other people's honesty is the kind of approach that will bring greater peace to all individuals and communities.

Each person's choice to engage in real communication is changing how the world communicates. And as big a statement as that is, it is as simple as returning to openness and honesty. Whenever you deviate, come back to what you've just learned.

In the next section you'll discover The Six Practices™, proven to increase your skills of openness and honesty and quickly return to real communication.

Here's a quick recap of what we've learned so far:

Honesty—being truly and freely yourself, speaking into what you want and how you feel.

Three Essentials

1. Truly and Freely You™
2. True Condition
3. About You

Openness—listening without reservation, putting your needs and wants on pause for someone else.

Three Essentials

1. Listen Without Reservation™
2. Taking It In and Letting It Go
3. About Others

Open + Honest = Real Communication

PART II

Introducing the Six Practices

6

The Agreement:
The Practice to Begin Real Communication

O ur first of the Six Practices, the Agreement, is a simple practice that will change the trajectory of any relationship you decide to use it in. This is how we bring real communication. It is a simple, powerful script to follow at the outset of any conversation. This is what gave us a solid foundation as we began working together.

Grace shares the following:

I first met Ken when he and Ilse brought little three-month-old Mila to the daycare where I was working. As we got to know their family, Ken's persistence that we be honest about Mila's day was, quite frankly, odd. We had been coached to "sandwich" any negative news and issues between the other positives of the day. To have a parent asking us to simply state what had happened was new territory for us.

As strange as it was at first, we came to love it. Knowing that Ken and Ilse were open to hearing how Mila's day *really* went meant that we could partner with them in a deeper way and help make Mila's transitions between home and school much smoother. Knowing that she had a rough day made it easier for them to understand when she was having a tough time at home and vice versa. Because of this, we developed a strong partnership with them. They rarely left the building without stopping to chat with us, even as Mila grew older and moved out of our infant room.

I received a voicemail from Ken about ten months after that first day. I knew he ran his own business from prior conversations. I had asked him multiple questions about his entrepreneurial journey. He said he was ready to hire an executive assistant and asked whether I was interested in the position. It took a little consideration, a few phone calls, and an informal interview, but eventually, we began working together.

As you can imagine, his push for honesty extended into how he did business as well. Before starting every meeting, he reminded me of the importance of honesty. He said it was the only way we'd accomplish things in a fast and clear manner. We agreed to be honest regularly. As we developed our work further, that eventually evolved into the Agreement. This was a new experience for me. Even though I had come from a family business—farming—and have had a job since the age of fifteen, running a business this way was not what I knew. Any meeting I had been a part of, *if* there were meetings in the first place, was simply the managers relaying information with little room for questions. My ideas and contributions never felt as if they were taken seriously. To suddenly be a part of the work and see my ideas come to life changed everything for me.

Because I was still working at the daycare at this time, I was going from a toxic culture to one I desperately wanted to experience more of. I tried to bring change into the daycare, even going so far as to write a letter to the then-CEO and owner. I explained the struggles we faced as employees and asked for a meeting to discuss them. We did have a brief meeting, but unfortunately these efforts did not make the transformation I had envisioned. There was little openness to the honesty I shared. I knew the desire for change ultimately had to come from the executive level, and that was unlikely to happen in my time of employment.

I reduced my hours with the daycare and took on more responsibilities with Ken to help get us to a point where I could join full-time. My focus was set on growing the company. It broke my heart to reduce my time and commitment to all the wonderful kids, but it was the right move for my future. I can only dream about what it would have been like to have more room for my honesty—the improvements we could have made and the impact on countless children as they grew under our care.

At the time of this writing, Ken and I have been working together for over six years. That is double the average tenure for someone my age. There was a time when I thought I'd be content as an executive assistant for the rest of my life, but our conversations have helped to push me far beyond what was once just a dream. I've taken on the responsibility of co-founder, strategic planning, clients, management, and much more. Openness and honesty are ingrained in everything we do, from how we speak to each other to the information we share with our clients. I've become a true partner in our business together and am committed to our mission. And it all began with an open and honest conversation.

The Agreement becomes especially helpful in setting expectations for what may be a difficult, challenging, or controversial discussion. You can use it in your personal and work lives with whomever you believe values openness and honesty and wants to have more moments of real communication. Here is the simple, powerful script:

The Agreement

"Will you agree with me on how we're going to communicate? I want you to be 100 percent honest, meaning be truly and freely yourself, speaking into what you want and how you feel. I promise you I will be 100 percent open to it. I will listen without reservation; I'll put my needs and wants on pause for you. In return, I will be honest with you, and I ask that you be completely open to it."

We use this precise approach, the Agreement, as a part of the healthy rules we share with all of our clients at the start of our work together. When we get the sense that someone is either not being honest or not being open, we simply point them back to the Agreement. Reminding someone of what they agreed to in the conversation and allowing them some grace to return to it ensures a better outcome for all. Because openness and honesty are skills to build, it will take constant reminders, at first, to come back to being open and honest. The goal is to remain in real communication throughout our discussions and disagreements. Our teams reach real communication and experience the highest levels of real relationships with team trust and psychological safety.

Beyond the session room, we also use the Agreement with all our third-party vendors. Here is the experience of Jeff Pipp, our social media vendor and partner:

> When we decided to work together, Ken kicked it off with the Agreement. At the time, I didn't think much of it, seeing it as a simple "yes" and easy enough to accomplish. I didn't fully experience the impact of that *yes* until further on in our relationship.
>
> For the first few weeks, it felt like the words "openness" and "honesty" were on repeat but not sinking into my head. I understood at a surface level what they were trying to do for people and communication, but I didn't understand the power behind those words initially.
>
> As our work progressed, I began to see what it meant to have the Agreement in place. I could really say what was on my mind, knowing that the person(s) on the other side, Ken and Grace in this case, wouldn't think less of me for it. That didn't mean they would like what I had to say or agree, but that they would listen, and I'd be heard. I found that it's about saying what you want with intention that makes our communication clearer. And I got that in return too. As a vendor to Know Honesty, I give honest feedback, knowing that our goals are aligned and any conflict serves to get us closer to achieving them.
>
> In contrast, I have other customers where the work feels more transactional and seems as though they're not willing to share the key ingredients and plans. It makes it harder on our side to distinguish what success means for them and how we can best serve

them as a third-party vendor. With Know Honesty, I feel like I'm on the team, and we, as a team, have the same goal.

It's extended past our relationship, too, into my career. In the last eight years of my professional life, and before I even met Ken and Grace, I've made intentional efforts to be more honest with moderate levels of success. But the idea of openness was tougher to understand.

In the past, I'd run into certain individuals and personality types that would frustrate me to no end. I struggled to understand their point of view and, as a result, would end up with a strained relationship and communication. By better understanding openness and practicing it, I've learned how to give others the platform to say what's on their mind and just listen to it while not actively disagreeing with it right away in my mind. I don't have to solve their problem immediately or convince them to take a different approach.

I understand now that I don't have to agree with them to be able to listen and hear where they're coming from. My initial response has shifted from "that's hogwash" to now first thinking, "I wonder why they think that?" That pause has helped me be less reactive, and I've had better conversations because of it. I feel more relaxed in those situations, knowing that I don't have to agree with them to still listen well and understand them better.

For our part, having the Agreement in place with Jeff means we're able to have such a high level of real communication that anything goes. He pushes back on ideas we have, explaining best practices for the industry without fear of losing us as a client. We get better results because of this, and our team mentality and partnership strengthen.

When first using the Agreement, it may feel awkward, and that is expected. We're taking that first step in asking for and creating real communication. Push past the discomfort and do it anyway because the communication and relationship on the other side far outweigh the awkward ten to fifteen seconds of stating the Agreement. You will need to repeat the Agreement several times until openness and honesty become the normal mode of communication rather than the rarity.

Ken shares how he has used the Agreement:

I recall needing a heavier dose of the Agreement when working with Truscott Rossman. Allie Walker, president, and John Truscott, CEO, were both passionate about the direction and vision of the organization. But the two couldn't agree on how to handle a prospective client. John overtly wanted them, Allie pragmatically didn't. The two strong-willed leaders began to defend their viewpoints. They were both trying to win the disagreement and in ways that hurt their ability to communicate.

When Allie disagreed with John wanting to onboard the client, he would simply push past her with his ideas. He wasn't respecting her stance, her expertise, or her opinion. Likewise, John didn't feel listened to or respected by Allie and thought, "Why deal with the tension when I could just press on?" To some degree, Allie would enable John to push past without expressing her complete disagreement and full feelings on the topic. John, being enabled to push past, was prepared to continue as he always had.

This relationship was far from being toxic or broken; rather, these were two people who cared deeply about one another and the organization. They were two people who struggled to communicate freely.

The tension wasn't just audible; it was physical. John wouldn't look at Allie directly, missing the WTF look on her face. John wouldn't look to see it, and Allie wouldn't speak to share it. Since Allie was giving 50 percent of her honesty, and John was about 50 percent open to Allie, we were operating with only half of their ability to create real communication. The conversation was lagging with no resolution in sight.

I butted in on the conversation: "We need to stop at this point. I don't think we are getting clarity on how you both feel and think on this one. I want us to approach this a bit differently. Allie, I want you to be 100 percent honest, truly, and freely yourself here, speaking into what you really want and how you feel about the topic. John, I want you to be completely open and listen without reservation. Put your needs and wants on pause to understand her viewpoint. Then, John, be completely honest back, and Allie, be completely open to it. Allie, your complete honesty, please."

Allie let it rip. She shared how she felt about the prospect of being wrong for the company and how she felt about John refusing to listen to her opinions. John looked at her during the exchange, lowering his guard and visibly listening. You could feel the emotional release from Allie and the vulnerability from John. As the two put everything on the table, they ultimately decided to disengage from the client.

As the rest of the meeting took place, Allie and John communicated with ease despite the hot, controversial topics. Ensuing sessions have taken place since that conversation, and the two are communicating with some of the highest levels of openness and honesty I have ever seen. As for the prospect, it turned out to be the right decision. Had the two decided not to engage in the conversation, that prospect would have been onboarded and become a threat to their business and reputation.

There are two valuable lessons within this story. The first is the sheer power behind communicating with complete openness and honesty. In this case, real communication led to better decision-making, a stronger relationship, and clarity on the true condition. The second is that the Agreement's simple approach created a clear path for two people to be truly and freely themselves and listen to one another in a way that's had transformative outcomes—and all it took were a few moments to voice, understand, and agree to it.

We recommend using the Agreement in any key relationships. Here are a few specific examples:

- At the beginning of any new relationship, whether in your personal or work life, use the Agreement to guarantee a stronger foundation from the outset. The alternative is having to go back and fix the relationship after toxic ways of communicating have taken root.

- In any recurring meeting, use the Agreement to establish expectations upfront. This will save you and your teams from wasting valuable time hunting down the true condition and guarantee you're solving the real problems quickly.

- Recall when we discussed family and long-standing relationships. Consider what the relationships in your life might be like today had they started out with the Agreement. Though we don't get an opportunity to travel back in time, the Agreement can and should be used within those relationships to begin the transformation toward a real relationship.

Grace shares a personal story:

When it comes to family and long-standing friendships, I have one that counts for both. I let gossip get the best of me and spoke disparagingly about a friend and family member of mine. I deeply disagreed with the choices she was making about building a home on family land but chose not to approach her with my thoughts. I had decided for her that she wouldn't be open to what I had to say and, therefore, felt justified in foregoing any attempt at communication. But my comments found their way to her without my knowledge.

She called me, already in a heated emotional state, and while I wish I could say I remained levelheaded, my anger and indignation quickly took over. I went on the attack in response. The conversation quickly devolved from there. Both of our walls soared high as we hurled hurtful jabs back and forth, such as, "You just don't know what you're doing" or "Well, you never took the time to understand and started judging." My entire body clenched tightly as we interrupted each other repeatedly. The conversation ended in tears on both sides, and I hung up with a pit in my stomach, knowing we had just destroyed the small amount of trust we had left.

A day later, I received a text from her stating she had "lost respect for me." The air left my lungs, and tears sprang into my eyes. I took it with malicious intent and knew we couldn't leave it at that as friends and family members; this relationship would continue for all our lives. Letting the hurt and words fester without any resolve would end up in hatred. For me, that was an unacceptable outcome. And so, a few days later, I found myself in a conversation that desperately needed to happen, and I knew would be unpleasant.

This time, we met face-to-face with a mediator included. I walked in with shoulders stooped, uneasiness flowing through my bones. She entered not long after, her face drawn closed and arms crossed. Seated on opposite sides of the kitchen table with our bodies angled away from each other, I began the conversation with the Agreement. I knew my actions that led to this point were wrong, and I was ready to take ownership of them. But the discomfort sat heavy in my throat and threatened to block our repair and reconnection. In using the Agreement, I knew we'd need that commitment to begin and revisit it multiple times.

The conversation lasted nearly three hours, filled with tears, eye rolls, and repeated apologies. Honesty was flying with brutality, and our mediator stepped in over and over to bring the emotions back down. At one point, I felt I had exhausted all the ways I could apologize and knew that her walls were up again. I asked her, "What else do you want? I think I've said all that I can, and right now, it doesn't feel like you're open to what I'm saying."

She paused, genuinely hearing what I said. She responded with, "I don't see how we can move past this now. It's not like I'm going to forget what you did." Finally, her honesty was on the table, and now we could work on moving forward. I considered her perspective and understood the challenge we faced together.

She was right; we'd have to rebuild the foundation of our relationship from scratch or live the rest of our lives with a hollow, fake connection at every family gathering. I replied, "One day at a time and conversation by conversation. I was wrong to not be honest with you in the first place, and look at where it landed us. We've both said some pretty hurtful things, and now we have to reestablish how we communicate together, but I'm willing to do it if you are because I love you and I care about you." She nodded and right there began a new version of our relationship.

Each time I look at her, I am grateful for her willingness to continue walking through life together. Even when we screw up and think it is beyond repair, one more conversation armed with openness and honesty will change the course of what otherwise would be lost. It takes courage, commitment, and continuous work on our communication skills to create and maintain healthy relationships that last a lifetime. Because what else do we really have at the end of the day?

Using the Agreement as often as possible creates a faster on-ramp to openness, honesty, and real communication, which breeds a higher level of trust much faster than what is otherwise possible. The Agreement reduces the time needed to create real relationships. It puts more intention and attention on our communication and our relationships. When you have it established and agreed to, it becomes easier to point back to the purpose of the conversation. The Agreement serves as a way to call out ourselves and others when we inevitably stray from being 100 percent open and honest.

Our Challenge for You:

Use the Agreement in three conversations this week and watch as real communication manifests before your eyes.

7

The Pursuit of Honesty® Assessment: *The Practice to Know Your Numbers*

We have been on our pursuit of changing how the world communicates for many years now. As it has evolved, we've noticed a growing need for data to track and understand our progress. People wanted the ability to assess and put numbers to where they stood with their skills of openness and honesty. And so The Pursuit of Honesty Assessment (PoHA) was born. It is the measurable approach to openness and honesty.

By answering a set of introspective questions, you'll receive the real-time data on your current levels of openness and honesty to understand your current ability to receive and deliver real communication. We've broken down the results by the overall score, your personal life, and your work life. By knowing where you stand, you'll know what areas of your life need the most attention. From there, you can take what you've learned in this book and work on increasing your percentages to create real communication and experience real relationships.

The purpose of this practice is to take an intangible, complicated topic and distill it down to figures and real data. The statistics we provide are only some of the initial findings as we continue our research. We are putting the numbers to good use by giving people the ability to make openness and honesty measurable. Until now, the world has not had a productive way to measure openness and honesty together. After all, humans love to measure. How long is this book? What time is it? How long before I arrive at work? How much coffee is left in my cup? To be a true master of communication, it is important that we not only give you the philosophy but also the appropriate data.

Personal Life vs. Work Life

As a part of your assessment results, we break your overall scores down into your personal life and work life. And here's why:

At a high level, there are often two modes of time in which we spend most of our day. We are either in the mode of our work life or our personal life. Your work life is spent putting your talents to work by producing, achieving, and contributing to an organization. Your personal life often has a different tone and broader spectrum of how you show up. Undeniably, the two are distinct yet inextricably linked. How we show up as open and honest is crucial to the organization's success and the outcomes of our personal lives.

When it comes to your personal life, at times, you'll find similarities with people. Enjoy them and use real communication to create a real relationship. And when you uncover differences, appreciate them. Those are opportunities for the two of you to learn from each other's experiences. You don't have to accept the differences, but you can at least take the time to understand someone else's journey and how they've come to be who they are. Appreciate their story and the differences created from it.

When it comes to the other side, one could make a case that being open and honest is easier in our work lives. The relationships are often newer and are goal-oriented, so the direction they're heading is clear. It may take less energy to work through issues because decisions are being made based on common objectives. We don't always have that in our personal lives, whether just meeting someone or in a longer relationship. When you find common goals with team members, solidify them and use them as building blocks. And when you uncover workplace differences, use open and honest communication to understand the true condition and move forward aligned.

We find that when working with clients, their personal lives seem to weave their way into our time together. We emphasize to the team that we're together to create stronger communication for the organization, but what they share and where they need to take the conversation is up to them. Without fail, we find ourselves talking about what's going on at home and how that affects their day-to-day work lives.

Grace tells the following story:

This comes as no surprise to me as a woman constantly in conversation with other women in leadership. We talk about bringing our full selves to work and the struggles of juggling parenthood, careers, and relationships. Women are leading the charge in having these conversations but men, on the other hand, seem to have been silent on this topic and are just now stepping up to add their voices and honesty too. They experience similar frustrations but often lack the space to talk about them.

In one of my workshops, I found myself with an all-male leadership team. Looking back, I can see now that I walked into that room holding some preconceived notions that they might see our work as "soft skills" and not be as engaged or that they'd keep the conversations strictly to their work and business outcomes. But as our time progressed, they proved me wrong and highlighted a need for continuous work on my own openness.

As the team grew closer, they shared honestly about their struggles within their homes, with their employees, and in previous experiences, each finding parts of their own lives within the stories. One of the questions I asked was, "What do you need to be honest about with this team here today?" We went around the table as each one shared until we got to the last person, Calvin.

As the general manager, Calvin was responsible for holding the rest of the team accountable and ensuring the plan was executed well. Outside of work, he was also a husband and dad with young kids, like the rest of his team. I looked to him as the pillar of the group, and what he shared embodied what leadership is evolving towards. He looked down at what he had written and then up to the team and said, "Life at home is about to get hectic. My stress level is rising due to the two kids and my wife about to give birth. She's on bed rest now, and she's having surgery after the delivery, too, so everything is falling on me right now. What I need from this team is simplification and little added stress."

By being honest in that moment, Calvin gave his team a peek into his everyday life and the opportunity to step up and share his burden of leadership for a time. Rather than trying to push on and hold back from the team until his breaking point, he took a step of trust, knowing that the men to his right and left would not see that as a weakness but a show of strength and belief in them as leaders. He knew they had a high ability to be open. In asking for the support he needed in the coming quarter, he also gave the team more clarity on his current reasoning and state of mind.

As much as we might wish otherwise, the joys and burdens of our personal lives often cross over into work and our ability to put our talents to use. There is no switch to flip as we settle into our workday that turns off all thoughts of what's going on at home. A simple acknowledgment, a moment of honesty, allows us to no longer hide from that reality. From there, we can then make better, more informed decisions and plans as they relate to our work lives.

After completing the assessment and receiving your percentages, it will be clear to you how you show up for yourself and everyone else in your life. Upon receiving your results, you can begin to work on what or who stands between you and being 100 percent open and 100 percent honest. Taking the Pursuit of Honesty Assessment every six months will show you the progress you are making on Your Pursuit (more on that in Chapter 11) and prompt deeper introspection as needed. The correlation between getting what you want and your ability to be open and honest is heavily tied. We encourage you to take the Assessment alongside those close in your life to accelerate Your Pursuit and deepen the richness of your conversations with those you care about. And in your work life, invite your team to take the Assessment and share results with one another. The conversation will uncover barriers that are standing in the way of making progress for your organization.

The Data

Through our research, we've discovered that people find themselves being more open and honest in one part of their life and less in the other. As we live out these two major pieces of our lives, we ought to make the most out of them. We must consider how we can be truly and freely ourselves and continue to listen without reservation at work and in our personal lives. If there is an imbalance between your work and personal life results, this will help you be more surgical in your approach to openness and honesty. This valuable data is a clue to where in your life you've lost confidence or clarity or live with an unhealthy amount of control, stress, and anxiety. Targeting where you struggle allows you to have a better focus on improving that area of your life.

When you take the Assessment with others, you can compare how someone might struggle with openness to your overbearing honesty or how someone is unable to be honest because you are frequently closed off to them. With the goal of developing a more real relationship and moving toward 100 percent in all areas, you can overcome these frequent challenges.

Including the stories in this book, we've witnessed hundreds of people graduate from only serving self to encouraging others to step into their greatness and embrace who they truly and freely are. It's one of the most rewarding things to be a part of and a glimpse of hope for our greater society.

A few trends we'd like to share based on our data analysis:

- As an individual's honesty increases, their openness increases at approximately the same rate.
- Age does not determine openness or honesty.
- On average, people are more open at work than in their personal lives.
- Openness and honesty peaks for those earning $100k to $150k but begins to fall again as income continues to rise.

- Personal honesty and work openness significantly influence life satisfaction. More so than age, gender, education, or income.
- On average, people are more honest in their personal lives than at work.
- Higher levels of openness and honesty tend to correlate to higher levels of life satisfaction.[5]

Through these statistics, you can clearly see what we've always known deep down: the more open and honest the collective, the better life experience overall.

Open and Honest Model

Having the above data is great, but now let's take the results even further by applying it directly to your life. For this next section, you'll want your individual results and those of your team as you apply them to your organization. To complete the Assessment, visit KnowHonesty.com/Assessment. It will take about ten minutes, then return to this page.

Based on your scores, find where you are on the model:

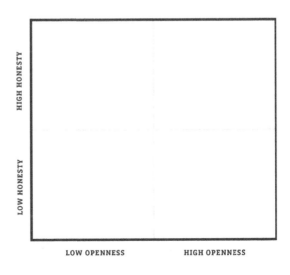

123

A few questions for you to consider before we explain the model and what it means:

Did your results surprise you? Why or why not?

What stands between you and 100 percent honesty?

What stands between you and 100 percent openness?

The Open and Honest Model is an efficient method to understand the different experiences we have with people in each category and, therefore, how they might experience us as well, based on where we land. The goal is to live within the High Honesty and High Openness quadrant as often as possible. At the top right of that quadrant is where the Agreement exists between two people.

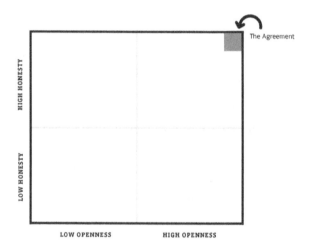

As we go through each quadrant, keep this question in mind: "What is it like to experience someone in this quadrant?" At different times in our lives, we show up in each one of these quadrants, shifting between all of them. Your scores from the Pursuit of Honesty Assessment tell you where you show up a majority of the time, but we all fluctuate throughout the quadrants. By understanding where we're at, we can more quickly shift back into that top right quadrant and experience all the positives that come with it. Knowing where you and others land will give you awareness as to how you experience one another and determine the path towards being 100 percent honest and 100 percent open.

Beginning with the Low Openness and Low Honesty quadrant, on the lower left, our experience of someone here shows that they are oblivious, disengaged, untrustworthy, and unreliable. And those who show up in this quadrant most of the time experience greater levels of isolation, anxiety, and loneliness. The awareness of how you are experienced will compel you to move to a more open and honest lifestyle. As we continue, we'll share the practices to help you move into the top right quadrant.

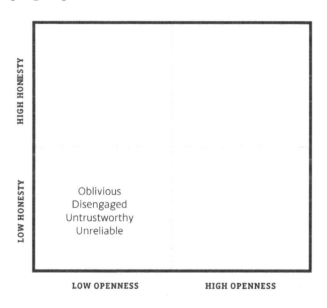

Next, let's look at High Honesty but Low Openness (upper left). We often experience someone with scores in this quadrant as being aggressive, defensive, arrogant, and disregarding others. Unfortunately, this is how many individuals experience people in leadership positions. Employees feel that leadership is handing down directives without understanding how they affect the rest of the organization. Someone within this quadrant has an impeccable ability to share who they are and speak about what they want and feel, but do so while dominating the room.

Take, for instance, those who are stubborn and steadfast in their beliefs. They cannot fathom why another person would believe anything different and are unwilling to hear the experiences that led others to a different conclusion. The situation becomes a dictatorship where collaboration dies, and other people's ideas go unspoken. Many factors trigger this behavior, and it creates frustration and division. When we remain in this quadrant, we inhibit connection and our ability to do better together.

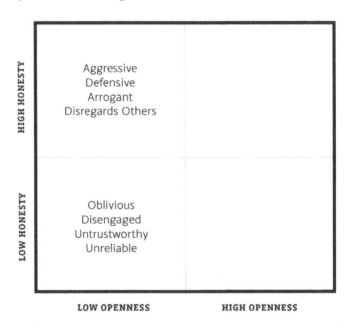

Moving on to the next quadrant (lower right), let's look at what it's like for someone who is High Openness but Low Honesty. Here, we see an individual as passive, stagnant, insecure, and indecisive. Think about someone who listens well and asks great questions but rarely shares their opinion and perspective. When working in a team toward a decision, this slows us down and blocks us from creating the best solution. We're unable to access the true condition because we're missing critical honesty, such as Cassie in Chapter 3 when the team needed to find a solution for recruiting. Knowing where a person stands when they remain in this quadrant is next to impossible and blocks us from any chance of creating real communication.

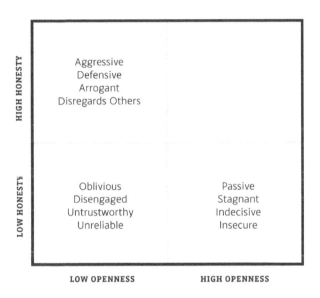

Often, the High Honesty, Low Openness individuals catch all the attention. It's easy to see why we actively complain about and avoid that person. We've heard people who show up in that quadrant called loudmouths or attention seekers. Their ability to be heard means we're more aware of them and less able to hear from others in the conversation. But someone who is Low Honesty, High Openness is harder to spot because they're unwilling to share their honesty, much less be heard. They are often described as people pleasers. But the issue is that they rob us of the opportunity for real communication at the same level as our person in High Honesty, Low Openness. If you put these two polar opposite individuals in a room, you can expect a massive gap in communication. Again, the goal is to move into the top right quadrant.

Let's enjoy the last quadrant, which is High Honesty and High Openness. This is where teams and relationships thrive. We experience someone within this quadrant as engaging, high trust, clear and actionable, and having an ease of communication. We've even had clients suggest that an individual like this is attractive in nature. When surrounded by people who reside in this quadrant much of the time, our lives become easier to navigate and, in the end, more enjoyable. Our real relationships are more concrete. We're quicker to identify the real problems and are equipped to solve them faster. When you meet someone else who lives in the top right quadrant, you will feel a sense of belonging. There will be two human beings willing to be fully honest and fully open with one another. These are the moments we want for everyone.

	LOW OPENNESS	HIGH OPENNESS
HIGH HONESTY	Aggressive Defensive Arrogant Disregards Others	Engaging High Trust Clear and Actionable Ease of Communication
LOW HONESTY	Oblivious Disengaged Untrustworthy Unreliable	Passive Stagnant Indecisive Insecure

At the start of this book, we talked about the flow of water. In the upper right quadrant, we create communication that is unhindered, untainted, and flowing purely back and forth. There are no disruptions because someone is completely open. There is no guesswork or lack of clarity because someone is completely honest.

Remember that we all will shift through these quadrants multiple times in our lives. It's not about only being in the High Honesty High Openness quadrant all the time, but more about recognizing when we're in the other quadrants and moving back toward 100 percent openness and honesty, pursuing that higher state of mind. And when you have the Agreement in place with someone else and notice when they may have shifted, you can invite them back into High Honesty and High Openness. The Agreement practice helps people show up in the top right quadrant with more frequency. The more people accept and live into the Agreement, the more they will naturally show up as High Honesty and High Openness.

As you commit yourselves to the top right quadrant, use your Pursuit of Honesty Assessment scores as a benchmark to navigate through your relationships and create real communication. We recommend retaking the Assessment every six months to understand yourself, where you're at, and how you've changed. Take

> The more people accept and live into the Agreement, the more they will naturally show up as High Honesty and High Openness.

it with a partner or your team to understand where you're at collectively when it comes to communication and learn where the current gains are to be made. The beauty isn't from the Assessment alone; it's in the conversation you have after. The next two practices we'll discover, Fake You and The Wall, will accelerate those gains and get you closer to being 100 percent open and 100 percent honest.

This simple approach is accessible to every single person, so lean in. Working on more openness and honesty in our lives is not a luxury reserved only for the rich, famous, and C-suite. It is for the individual ready to commit to being truly and freely themselves and, in turn, wanting it for everyone else around them.

Our Challenge for You:
Encourage three people in your life to take the
Pursuit of Honesty Assessment and guide them through
their results using the Open and Honest Model.
Remember, the beauty is in the conversation.

8

Fake You: *The Practice to Level Up Your Honesty*

E arlier, we shared how one of our clients answered the question, "If you are not the real you, who are you?" Those who answered "fake" were spot-on. And that brings us to the third of the Six Practices: Fake You. Fake You is the façade we project rather than being 100 percent honest, truly and freely ourselves.

It's not you at your core. It disguises who we really are, how we think, what we want, and how we feel. It is a complete blockade to honesty. When we're projecting Fake You, we're unable to be in the High Honesty quadrant on the Open and Honest Model and can no longer participate in the Agreement. It is the gap we must overcome to achieve a higher level of honesty. We must rid ourselves of Fake You.

> **Fake You is the façade we project rather than being 100 percent honest, truly and freely ourselves.**

Ken shares the following story:

Early in my professional career, I worked for an organization selling insurance to people I didn't believe needed it. This weighed on me and bothered me. Yet, I continued on. I set out to please the powers that be and worked around the clock to meet my goals. Unfortunately, I was good at selling and hitting targets. Fake You was taking a permanent place in my life with every successful sale.

I sold this product every day and felt my skin crawl as I became a liar, fraud, and fake just to feed my own financial benefit. I was making more money than I ever had made before, but it left me uncomfortable and misaligned within myself. It's an evil twist to keep doing something you believe is wrong but being paid handsomely doing it. The façade I had to keep up was taking a toll on my soul.

Over time, Fake You wore on me enough to exit the organization. The peace that came with no longer being required to fake it was well worth leaving behind that paycheck. I shed that Fake You at work and moved on to something more aligned with myself and my pursuit.

Unfortunately, it's difficult to avoid Fake You altogether in this life. Thus, we must equip ourselves to recognize it quickly. Early on, this is a reflective practice, but as you become more familiar with Fake You, you'll sense it rising in the moment and be able to rid yourself of it immediately. Fake You presents itself in different ways for each person, but below are ten common scenarios to watch out for as you begin:

1. You say, "I'm fine," but you aren't.

2. You accept a leadership promotion, but you can't stand leading people.

3. You say, "I love you," when you actually don't.

4. You spend time with people pretending to enjoy their friendship.

5. You tell someone, "This is great work!" but know you'll need to redo it.

6. You pretend your relationship with a family member has no issues.

7. You have an emotional outburst that doesn't reflect who you are.

8. You regret hurting someone, but move on as if nothing happened.

9. You know you're wrong but continue on anyway.

10. You desperately want to try something different but instead maintain the status quo.

Think about where else Fake You has occurred in your own life. Use the space below to list three instances. Naming them alone will create great awareness in your life. Please take a couple of minutes now to do so.

1. _____

2. _____

3. _____

Reflecting on these answers, ask yourself: Why did Fake You surface?

1. _____

2. _____

3. _____

Know there are thousands of different answers to the question why. No one reason is better or worse. Your reasons are uniquely yours, but we must move past them to get rid of Fake You. Below we've answered why from each of the above scenarios through our own lens.

You say, "I'm fine," but you aren't. Why? Because I didn't want to share a weakness or struggle.

You accept a leadership promotion, but you can't stand leading people. Why? My eyes were on the money, not aligned with what I wanted to do.

You say, "I love you," when you don't. Why? I'm attempting to avoid hurting someone else.

You spend time with people pretending to enjoy their friendship. Why? I thought it'd be a distraction and maybe some connection, but I ended up feeling more distant.

You tell someone, "This is great work!" but know you'll need to redo it. Why? I wanted to avoid conflict to protect myself.

You pretend your relationship with a family member has no issues. Why? I don't have the courage to take an opposing stance.

You have an emotional outburst that doesn't reflect who you are. Why? My emotions got the best of me before I could pause for a moment.

You regret hurting someone, but move on as if nothing happened. Why? I'm afraid of what they'll say to or about me.

You know you're wrong but continue on anyway. Why? It's too embarrassing to admit I'm wrong.

You desperately want to try something different but instead maintain the status quo. Why? My self-doubt keeps me from even trying.

Each answer represents the shell of ourselves, one where we're alive but not truly living as we were intended. Hiding behind Fake You blocks us from taking risks and participating fully in this one life we've been given.

Recall Gino Wickman's story from Chapter 3. He was expending enormous amounts of energy being someone he wasn't with each group. That is happening to each one of us too. This leaves you with less time, energy, and space to pursue what you really want in life. Every time we project Fake You, we lose some of our precious energy because it is being sapped away by holding up that façade. Instead, imagine what more could be achieved with that energy directed toward our goals and relationships.

For leaders of organizations, consider what your employee experience is like when it comes to Fake You and their work lives. If the environment you've created or been handed is not one where everyone is able to be open and honest, Fake You is likely happening everywhere. And when someone must both maintain a façade and perform at work, their performance will suffer every single time.

Ken shares how a client dealt with Fake You:

I remember a moment with one of my clients, Truck and Trailer Specialties. This is a family-owned business, with the patriarch, Dan Bouwman, at the helm. At the time, the leadership team consisted of Dan, his brother Mark, his two sons Brian and Mike, his grandson Brad, and their HR director, the only non-family member of the team. Dan has a bear of a voice and the presence of a bull, the kind of attitude straight out of a movie. And that's just Dan; every other person is unique and full of personality too. They had pushed through some of the most difficult circumstances any company could ever imagine. This time around, the seasoned and emboldened team was upon yet another significant challenge. Like other companies at this time, they were struggling with the ability to recruit great talent in a post-COVID world.

It seemed the Great Resignation was hitting them, and it impacted everyone's psyche.

Before we discuss their challenge, you must know one of their most important core values is "Exceptional Work Ethic with Grit." They built their company on this principle. It is how they hire people, fire people, and hold each other accountable every single day.

The team and I began to discuss the pain point. The tension in the room was high, given the severity of the circumstances. After a bit of discussion among the team, we hadn't come up with any immediate resolution to the absence of talent. They needed to fill a significant amount of positions in the coming quarter to continue providing their current level of service. I shared various trends and approaches: unlimited PTO, flexible working hours, the four-day workweek, and various employment benefits that other companies had deployed. As I continued, the silence became a bit eerie. And then, it got a little more tense.

Dan, awaiting his moment to respond to all the ideas, slammed his fist on the table. He said, "You know what needs to happen? These f***ing millennials need to starve!"

I thought I was about to lose control of the room. The fist slam left a wake; his words were stern and intentional. My walls immediately went up. After all, I'm one of those "f***ing millennials." I thought, "Is he really being open to the ideas?" I almost interjected to soften the blow and ease the room, but I paused for a moment. I was the one not ready to be open. I had to first lower my walls to listen to the message Dan was about to share. He wasn't letting Fake You take over by pretending to nod and agree with my suggestions.

After a brief silence, he continued in his bearish tone, "I saw the same thing in the seventies. Hippies didn't want to work, and it did them no good. And here we sit again, experiencing the same cycle."There was only one other person in the room, Mark, who could relate to the experience in the seventies. Even so, the entire team understood the context of the statement.

Dan persisted as the team listened intently. "We aren't going to be the company that rides the wave of the latest trend. If we do that, then we aren't living 'Exceptional Work Ethic with Grit.'" He laid his point on the table. The rest of the team chimed in, some disagreeing and others agreeing. It was a passion-filled conversation in all the best ways. They spoke and listened with the intent to hash out the best, next right thing to do for the company. The conversation was honest, not one Fake You to be seen at that table. And on the other side, the team was open to one another's viewpoints.

Ultimately, Dan and the team decided to double down on their recruiting efforts, not bending to the latest business trends and embracing their own culture of grit. Dan's historical perspective really helped the team. They landed gritty employees and never wavered on their own core values. The long-term play proved to be beneficial, as their competitors and suppliers hired whoever they could get while adding excessive benefits. This hurt the other companies' cultures and productivity. Truck and Trailer Specialties stayed true to who they are, continually attracting like-minded employees and building on a foundation of Exceptional Work Ethic with Grit. Organizationally they chose to be truly and freely themselves despite the challenges.

Had I interjected or Dan reserved his honest opinion, the company may have irrevocably damaged their culture by hiring people who weren't committed to their core values, ultimately losing their company's honest self.

Truck and Trailer Specialties' discussion was a moment of real communication within a leadership team. The team members were honest, they said what they meant, and they listened to one another no matter how bold or brazen the communication. They didn't throw walls up. Instead, they kept them down to better understand each other. They engaged in as much communication as necessary to sort through the disagreements and fought to get on the same page, picking one path they could all align on.

That's real communication. And it felt remarkable to witness. When you do experience it, you may wonder why it doesn't happen more. See, that's the point—it should. And it can. Real communication isn't some theoretical unicorn we see only once in a blue moon. Rather, it is present and available to us all the time. It does, however, take work. Effort. Energy. Strategy. Self-control. All the things that often fall by the wayside when we don't communicate well. Understanding it is simple; executing it is something else.

Your commitment to honesty will be tested on a regular basis. There will be lazier, easier paths to choose than to be honest. It may happen consciously or unconsciously throughout the day. But know this: More times than not, that "easier" way will leave you feeling empty. Ridding yourself of Fake You creates real momentum to get you to what you want faster.

> **More times than not, that "easier" way will leave you feeling empty. Ridding yourself of Fake You creates real momentum to get you to what you want faster.**

With Fake You cast aside, you'll experience:

- Less pressure to conform to everyone else's expectations
- A natural, unshakeable confidence rooted in yourself
- Your life with more direction and meaning
- Ultimate clarity to identify real problems quickly
- Deeper, real relationships with those around you
- Better use of your energy when it's not directed toward upkeeping Fake You
- A sense of pride in simply being who you are.

Use this third practice to help clarify moments when you were not honest, understand why, and begin to recognize when Fake You surfaces in real-time. Now, focus on your honesty moving forward. Be truly and freely you, access the true condition, and keep it about you.

Once you've gotten more in touch with yourself, look outside yourself and help others do the same. Knowing and owning your struggles puts you in a great position to encourage others going through the same circumstance so that you can do better together.

Our Challenge for You:
Catch Fake You rising in the moment
and rid yourself of it.
Make note of when and why it happened,
and choose to return to honesty.

9

The Wall: *The Practice to Level Up Your Openness*

ow that we've covered how to become more honest by ridding ourselves of Fake You, we must address what blocks us from being open. This is our society's great challenge. It is The Wall. The Wall is the divide we create between ourselves and others rather than being 100 percent open, listening without reservation, putting our needs and wants on pause for someone else.

> **The Wall is the divide we create between ourselves and others rather than being 100 percent open, listening without reservation, putting our needs and wants on pause for someone else.**

This typically happens when we disagree, judge others, cast reservations, are challenged, or distracted. The Wall prevents us from being 100 percent open and closes us off from everyone else. Think about the last time you were frustrated with a political statement. Immediately, you put up a Wall. When a neighbor annoyed you with a conversation—Wall. Someone couldn't understand why you were so angry—Wall.

We construct all these walls. And every time we hit the Wall, it causes us and the other person pain and discomfort, leading to increased disconnection. So, we build more Walls, assembling our fortress, attempting to reject the blows that life inevitably delivers. But the more we build, the more unhappy we become, the more Walls we hit, and the more isolated we feel. We slowly become trapped, this time having placed ourselves in a very precise box with nowhere to move. When the Wall goes up, we're no longer able to live in High Openness on the Open and Honest Model and can't actively participate in the Agreement. To really connect, gain a deeper understanding, and engage in human interaction, we must break down the Wall.

Ken shares an example of the Wall:

I have served many clients over the course of my career. But out of all of them, there is one that epitomizes the Wall more than any others. That client remains my greatest nightmare. When you're in the open and honest business, a client who is argumentative, aggressive, and not listening leaves you with little ability to make any progress within the team. I've had clients who came close to losing everything because of their Walls. I've had people call each other's mother stupid. I've had clients who slammed the table, physically threatening someone because of what they said. But this one still takes the cake.

When this team of six showed up at my offices for their first day, we began to work through the EOS Process® (an operating system for managing all your team's human energy). I was immediately confronted with a mixed bag of attitudes. The owner came in pensive; her husband entered with a cold, unwelcoming demeanor, and the others seemed eager to watch it all play out, unwilling to speak up and telling me with their eyes that this was just another day at the office.

I reviewed the agenda as I started the session and asked everyone to check in with my standard questions. They all hastily started writing, except for the husband. He crossed his arms, making it as clear as possible that he didn't approve of something. I asked, "Are you ready to share?"

He responded gruffly, "I'm not enrolled."

I asked him again as if I didn't hear him.

He continued, "I'm not enrolled in this program."

The coldness in his voice and his sheer displeasure were on full display.

"But you're here, aren't you?" I said. "I mean, you know what the team is here to do."

Referring to his wife, he said, "She wants me to be here."

I went in a little farther. "I thought you were a part of this team, but if you don't want to be here, go ahead and exit and we will continue on."

His wife stepped in. "Ken, please continue. I want him to see this." She was looking at him as if to say, 'Why are you doing this to us?'

It killed me to watch this happen to a husband-and-wife team. I could only imagine what their exchanges might be like when I wasn't in the room. I deeply cared for the wife, and the rest of the team seemed like good-natured people, so I decided to forge ahead.

We powered through over the course of nine hours. And to my right, three feet away, was a man throwing a childlike tantrum the entire time. He only fought for himself and put a tall Wall between himself and everyone around him. This in-person isolation didn't only hurt us by not giving his full expertise, but it put everyone else on guard too. By the end of the day, I had exhausted my abilities to teach the team EOS® and help their company while also fighting to break through this man's Wall.

Before scheduling another session, I told the team I would need him to apologize to us all and then confirm he was committed to the process. As expected, he met that request with the same aggression he had demonstrated throughout the day. Not so shockingly, he refused to apologize. This company was sitting on a big solution to set them free, but instead, they passed it by because of one of the biggest, most stubborn egos I'd ever encountered.

The experience, as rattling as it was, gave us a range of lessons to learn. The sad truth is that human beings must deal with people who throw their Walls up all the time. It makes life difficult, and that's the problem with human beings and Walls. We want to serve self first and most often, sacrificing all the benefits other human beings can bring to the table.

In *Untethered Soul*, author Michael Singer says, "Pain and suffering come from our resistance to life events, period." Life is going to happen. It's going to present challenges, conflicts, difficulties, and differences to us no matter who we are or where we are. And rather than accept that, we put up the Wall and create massive divides between ourselves and everyone on this planet. We create unnecessary suffering and isolation for ourselves when we choose not to be open. The Wall becomes our resistance to reality. We live in conflict and disagreement with others, and that inevitably impacts our lives. Every time you throw the Wall up, you add to that chasm and create more stress upon yourself and your mind.

Now, that is not to say it's impossible to live life without Walls. In some ways, they are a response to threats, and we activate them as part of our fight-or-flight behavior. However, most of life should not be experienced staring at a Wall. Know that you'll find Walls everywhere; it behooves you to push them down with as much frequency as possible. In every office, every family, and any space where people have gathered, there will be Walls. Although we experience them as part of our lives, we cannot allow these Walls to block us from connecting with each other.

When we facilitate a conversation with leaders and managers, we are really looking for two things:

Is the person speaking being honest?
Are the people in the room being open to it?

Of the two, the easier one to spot is when people aren't being open. We'll often observe someone checking their phone, gazing off into the distance, silently fuming, or—our personal favorite—giving a straight-up eye roll. Each is an example of putting up a Wall. And in each instance, we immediately lose the ability to communicate in an open and honest way.

We've become so familiar with our individual Walls that we often don't even realize when they go up. Like when we dismiss someone's idea because their last one didn't work. Or when we don't engage in a political conversation because we know the other person sits on the other side of the aisle. So, we act as though nothing they have to say could possibly be relevant to us. That "aisle" is really another Wall in disguise, created to keep a divide between us.

From the mundane to the extreme, the Wall encroaches on our lives without us realizing it. It blocks us from being curious about another person, investigating a new idea, and seeing opportunities on the horizon. Each Wall keeps us stuck in the same pattern of thinking and limits our growth as an individual, an organization, and a society. Just think: If you weren't open throughout all of your education, you wouldn't grow. Life itself is one big giant school, yet we are refusing to learn.

If we can better recognize the Walls as they come up, we can more easily eliminate them immediately when they do. We need to lean into more openness, listen without reservation, and put our needs and wants on pause for someone else, even if for a brief moment. Moving past the Wall individually advances us all together.

The first step is to recognize what your Walls might look like and when they unknowingly present themselves. These are a few relatable Walls you might be able to recognize within yourself. Once you are aware of them, you'll find the Walls easier to identify and ultimately eliminate:

The Aggressive Wall: Imagine a wall with "FU" spray-painted on it. This is the type of Wall in which you are sending the most confrontational message possible without choosing to engage.

The "I'm Always Right" Wall: It seems "built-in" that we think we know better all the time. What would we gain from anyone else's perspective? Yet never understanding someone else means we never have access to the true condition. With awesome, flawless, and perfect you, why would there need to be room for anyone else?

The Nervous Wall: The moment something feels foreign to you, you hide rather than embrace the full experience.

The Busy Wall: Life seems to love busy, and when you are too busy, that leaves little room for anything else. Too much work life, less time for your personal life. Too much personal life, less time for work life. Put another way, The Miss Out on Life Wall.

The Mad Wall: When the Wall is on fire, burning high and hot, nothing can get through. Not only does it burn you, it burns others.

The Exhausted Wall: "I will lie down right here with my eyes closed, but I promise I'm listening." When we've exhausted ourselves, that leaves little energy for anyone else. (See the Busy Wall for why we're exhausted.)

The Control Wall: The moment you don't have the reins and someone else does, you attempt to build a wall to get back control. Before you know it, you're stuck with *all* those reins.

That is not an exhaustive list, but certainly some of the most common Walls we see. Every Wall is one that we have chosen to build, consciously at first, but now it appears immediately and without thought. We've crafted its size, weight, and thickness. We allow the Walls to grow, at times not realizing it because they have taken root in our subconscious. Whether we have a quick moment where the Wall pops up, or we have designed our entire life with layers upon layers of Walls, we did it. Our brains, at first, will resist the change to eliminate the Wall, wanting to cling to the status quo. But we can choose to rise above that and knock them down.

We've yet to find one Wall worthy enough to remain standing. And we would like to think we have seen them all. The big ones. The small ones. And nearly everything in between. They do not serve our best interests, do not progress or promote our goals, and often blur our future vision. Why would anyone, knowing that, want to keep these Walls up? The answer is an easy one: because our egos, emotions, fears, and judgment get in the way of progress.

Our Walls cause us unnecessary and extensive pain and suffering. The most heartbreaking situation is to live in isolation because of the Walls we've erected around ourselves.

Because the Walls have shifted to our subconscious mind, we must call them back into our conscious mind and evaluate them. That is not always an easy process, but with these practices, it is well within your reach.

We've worked with individuals who've experienced trauma at the hands of abuse and neglect and have found more freedom by knocking down their Walls to fully experience life. There are business owners demolishing their Walls daily in service of being a better leader to their people. We continue to encounter our Walls and have gotten to the point where we can send them down before they've even begun to rise. You, too, will reach that point with practice, focus, and commitment.

We must strive to live a life without Walls. Ridding yourself of them can offer the following benefits:

- Reduce anxiety
- Eliminate neurotic control
- Less "me, myself, and I" and more "we, us, and togetherness"
- Ease unhealthy aggression toward others, even yourself
- Experience more transformational ideas
- Limit constant judgment, reducing stress on you and others
- Build a stronger relationship, one that allows others to thrive in it
- Enjoy greater peace
- Enhance love and belonging

Think about when the Wall occurs in your own life. It usually comes in some form of resistance you can feel. Feel free to use the Wall examples from earlier in the chapter to help. Use the space below to list three instances in which the Wall has appeared. Give yourself a few minutes to do so.

1. _____

2. _____

3. _____

Reflecting on your answers, ask yourself why the Wall appeared.

1. _____

2. _____

3. _____

Below, Ken will share a few examples of the Wall in his life and tactics to eliminate them.

1. The "I'm Always Right" Wall appears. I can't stand people who have an insistent political bent and pushiness.

Why does this Wall appear? It annoys me, and I can see how the political pushiness possibly frustrates others. At times, their viewpoints are wrong and too extreme. Yet, I also can see I've really made this about me and not them. I have an egotistical need to be right.

Tactic: Make it about others. To eliminate this Wall, I make an effort to genuinely understand them. I pause my thoughts to hear their thoughts. I will proceed with my honesty at some point, but as of now, it's about them, not me. I find greater peace in the conversation, and we'll have a little more fun together because I'm not trying to oppress or change their mind.

2. The Control Wall appears. I get home, the house is a mess, and my wife has lost control of the situation. She expresses her frustration, and I begin to judge her abilities. I've heard enough and prepopulated my thoughts and criticism.

Why does this Wall appear? She seemingly can't handle everything, and I am disappointed things aren't done my way. This continues to happen, and I would have done it all differently. I'm frustrated she doesn't always heed my advice. I desire complete control.

Unfortunately, in this scenario, I am only seeing things through my own eyes. I have taken no time to understand her day or point of view. Because things weren't done my way, it's caused me to throw up my Wall.

Tactic: Listen without reservation. To eliminate this Wall, I'm going to "take in" the scenario as it is. I'm going to notice and hear my wife out. I'm going to seek to understand her pain. I'm going to look at more than just my narrow perspective on the situation. Maybe I'll even appreciate that my kids are having fun and have a renewed respect for my wife's hard work.

3. The Mad Wall Appears. A client tells me my approach isn't working. They proceed to send some slanderous comments my way.

Why does this Wall appear? It infuriates me that this client who has issues speaks to me this way. This approach would save his team, but instead, he cuts me down. I've done nearly everything I could to help him and his team, but in all actuality, I'm mad I didn't do more.

Tactic: Take it in and let it go. To eliminate this Wall, I recognize that I am fuming. I breathe to calm myself. I release my white-knuckle tension and do the best I can to hear what he is saying. There is a lesson here, and if I burn this relationship, I may never understand how to improve. The conversation ensues. My calm invites him to be calm, and my understanding gives him understanding. We both learn and grow better together.

In each of these instances, I had to take a moment to remember that it's not all about me and what I want. There are other people in my life, and they are not obligated to live solely based on my terms. Inevitably, a similar situation to those above will occur again. Because I've taken the time to reflect on some of my Walls and why they appear, I'm better prepared for the next occurrence. I walk into any situation knowing I can knock down my Walls and return to a state of clarity and togetherness. From that place, life becomes continuously more enjoyable.

If this work seems scary, it's because you are facing something new, sometimes difficult, and often much more challenging than just living in the status quo. We've all been there before. Just think about the first time you jumped off a diving board, attended a new school where you didn't know anyone, traveled to another country, or experienced something unfamiliar. Did you feel scared? Frightened? Hesitant? Of course, that is just your gut and brain taking over. It's human nature. We are often scared of the unknown, even if we have no reason to be. But we should really fear *fear* stopping us—from progressing, growing, and improving.

Fear is the blockade that stops us from having the full experience of life. Fear manifests itself in unique ways for every individual but is no less a real barrier that we all share and we all face. It prevents us from communicating well, from being ourselves, and from reaching our full potential.

When stepping into a room filled with people, we each have a moment of weakness when fear snags the opportunity to take root. For some, it comes in the form of not sharing and engaging. Fear whispers that we'll be safer in the corner, mute and uninviting, not taking the risk to be seen and known by others. Alternatively, for some, fear becomes a raging wave. It declares that their opinion must be heard above all else, lest they be thought less of.

Throughout the spectrum of how fear manifests itself, we lose sight of the humans in the conversation. We turn inward and protect ourselves to quell the fear that silently seeped in. We get stuck, missing the opportunities for progress and deeper relationships. This fear is simply another Wall.

There will always be some unpredictability when we encounter a new person. Because of this friction, we constantly throw space between ourselves and the people around us, no matter how much love we have for that person. This is ingrained in our evolution—taking a strong position on differences, casting people out of "our" world, as opposed to understanding how another person experiences the world we share. It is a method of protection on the surface, but it quickly becomes a path to isolation and self-serving.

Remember, a Wall is a nasty barrier between you and everyone else in your life. It threatens connection, steals years from you due to stress, and rips happiness from you. Consider what Walls you put up, consciously and unconsciously. We all benefit when we have fewer Walls between us, thus creating more room for everyone else in our lives. We have the power and ability within ourselves to shake off the Wall when it rises and choose an outward connection.

Our Challenge for You:
Catch the Wall rising in the moment
and quickly eliminating it.
Identify why it came up and
how you can return to openness faster.

10

The Still: *The Practice to Know Where You're At*

Most of the people we work with are fast-paced individuals. They are constantly pushing themselves to do better, be better, and achieve more. Their drive and nonstop motion have served them well in life until, suddenly, it doesn't. At some point, they stop and look around, only to find that they've created a life they don't enjoy. This next practice slows down that pace, if only for a moment, for a needed breath and reflection so we don't reach that point. It is called the Still. The Still helps you think, be present, and access the true condition.

It is designed to take you deeper into being open and honest, helping you uncover and become aware of where you're at today. We often don't take the time to understand where we're at in our lives as they play out. And because we leave little to no room for reflection, we end up coasting through life a bit directionless and uncertain.

> **The Still helps you think, be present, and access the true condition.**

Warren Buffet is credited with saying, "Busy is the new stupid." After hearing that, we noticed just how many of us, ourselves included, described our lives and calendars as "busy" without questioning why. We struggle to stop and consider what we're doing and the impact the constant hurry has upon us. In our time spent with individuals and leaders, we invite them to pause and evaluate themselves for just this reason.

Here is a story from Grace:

Tim had taken over the family business from his father several years before we met and had recently started another new business with a few people from his current leadership team. Outside of work, he was also a father, husband, brother, and friend. Suffice it to say, Tim had a lot on his plate.

Before the team completed the Still, we asked them to consider the following categories in addition to those already listed: company culture, team performance, employees, and company processes. Then, we sent them out of the room and gave them ten minutes of silence to contemplate and fill out the Still. Upon returning, we asked each person to share what they uncovered.

Tim came back into the room wiping away tears, and I could see the concern on his team members' faces. When it was his turn to share, he cleared his throat and said he hadn't expected to see so much discontent on the page, but as he considered each category, that number continued to grow. Seeing it on paper shifted all that discontent into reality, and he acknowledged all he had taken on.

When it came to the company culture and answering why he was discontent, Tim made a huge discovery. He found that he didn't like the current culture. It was the one that had been set decades back when his father still ran the business, and it continued on into today. He felt like he was still living in his dad's shadow, and as an unconscious response, he had started a new company, adding more to an already full life.

In ten intentional minutes, Tim pinpointed the major sources of his discontent and understood the reasons why. He found true power in knowing and sitting with the reality of what his life had become. First comes awareness, then comes action. For Tim, as a person of action, he now had an opportunity to continue on or make a change toward more peace and contentment in his life.

Think about your life as a movie. The Still takes a scene from the movie, where you're at today, and pulls it out as a static photograph. It captures the moment in a way that exposes the true condition and behind-the-scenes reality. When we take more time to understand our own Still and true condition, we better shape the outcome of our own movie.

Consider your life in terms of the Still. Where are you at this exact moment? What are the sources of your content and discontent? Use the worksheet below to crystalize each major category of life listed and others as needed. For each category, check whether you are content or discontent and list why you've chosen that answer. When answering why, do your best to go deep below the surface level.

Let's take friendship as an example. You may mark discontent and move to answering why. Your first thought may be, "I don't make enough time for my friends." But again, ask yourself why. "Because I prioritize work." Now, at this point, you could stop, but you know there's a deeper reason. Why? "Because we don't connect like we used to, and I'm afraid to bring that up." In that answer, you've hit the root of your discontent—fear of rejection if you try for a deeper connection.

Take the next ten minutes and complete the Still. If you are a leader of people, we encourage you to add the following categories for your work life: culture, people, process, and performance. Get clear and really focus on who you are right now. (To download additional copies of the Still, go to KnowHonesty.com/the-still.)

DATE:

CATEGORY	CONTENT	DISCONTENT	WHY:
Friendships			
Family			
Romantic			
Profession/Career			
Physical			
Mental			
Spiritual			
Living Conditions			
Knowledge/Education			
Finances			
Entertainment/Hobbies			

Once completed, take another moment to look at the Still as a whole. Notice the frequencies of your content and discontent categories. This is your true condition. You're now able to see how far you've come and where you stand today. Use the Still as your reflection practice. Learn from your past and enjoy the parts of your life that you're content with right now. You likely put in some hard work to get to a place of peace within that category of your life. Take a moment to recognize and celebrate.

Because you have your first completed Still, your path forward is now easier and clearer. In Chapter 11, you'll experience and enjoy forging ahead—as *you*. We'll discuss ways to bring forth more contentment in your life. Keep this Still as you evolve into the future; you'll want to reflect on how far you've come. We recommend revisiting the Still every six months to keep a pulse on your changes and growth.

Using the Still in Teams

When it comes to organizations, we often reflect with our clients to help them center on the true condition of their organization. One client, SJA Solutions, had such a great moment doing exactly this. Sean Agerson, the visionary, and Kevin Trapp, the integrator, have come against challenge after challenge in their organization. Not just the normal business hiccups; we are talking about massive challenges. They've faced leadership exodus, the global pandemic, a sales dry spell to overwhelming sales, and everything in between. These challenges have crushed organizations before, but SJA Solutions has mastered reflecting on the true condition. They have the ability to cut through all the noise and land on the root issue.

Ken shares the following example:

I recall one of our session days working through their last quarter, and they were frustrated with what they hadn't achieved. There was ample opportunity for drama, complaints, and aimless discussion. Instead, after some brief commiserating, they quickly turned the discussion into focusing on the top issues and uncovering their discontent. I had them pause and take a few quiet minutes to reflect on the root of this discontent. I encouraged them to go deep and push on *why*. Once they had done this, they each shared for a few minutes. We found the source of the frustration was two-pronged: their recruiting was not executing well, and their training wasn't quick and educational enough. They sifted through the noise and called out the top culprits of their discontent quickly, not by continually discussing it but by taking just a few moments to reflect.

From there, the team began to deep dive into each topic, focusing on the more pressing recruiting issue. They began answering the *why* to their discontent and getting clear on the issue. Kevin started by saying they weren't focused on it enough. Sean added that no one was owning it, leading to ambiguity around responsibility. Furthermore, the team admitted they didn't have expertise on the matter. They leaned into their honesty to expose the true condition. They tapped into their openness, genuinely interested in one another's perspectives. They got real about their situation. SJA Solutions was getting clear on their Still as an organization.

As a result of their newfound clarity, they enhanced their recruiting efforts, created a clear owner of recruiting, and began having a successful pipeline of talent. None of this would have been as easy had they not taken the time to pause, reflect, and target the source of their struggles.

Our Journey with You

At times, the Still is filled with contentment for both of us, and we're blessed to be able to say that. Yet, some categories sit in discontentment. Without this practice, identifying the source and understanding why becomes a monumental feat. All of us have so much going on that we get lost in the weeds quickly and forget to reflect on what is going well and what isn't.

We'll discuss how to take action in the next chapter, but for now, simply sit with the Still. Acknowledge the categories of discontent and know that it's possible to shift them toward content. As for the content categories, recognize and celebrate each one. There was likely a time in your life when that was not the case. Create a moment for gratitude and you'll find those categories will grow ever stronger.

Our Challenge for You:

Carve out time each week for stillness and reflection.
Use the Still to check in with yourself and
the true condition every six months and
celebrate the evolutions of you.

11

Your Pursuit: *The Practice to Know Where You're Going*

C huck Palahniuk wrote in *Fight Club*, " If you don't know what you want, you end up with a lot you don't." We can apply this quote to so many people who have come and gone in our lives. From close friends destroyed by numbing addictions to companies whose leadership lost its way. When we look at how this relates to openness and honesty, we know that someone with low levels of both is often oblivious and disengaged. There is a lack of direction because there has been no focus on their life and getting what they want from it. For those who don't want to fall into that trap, we've created Your Pursuit.

Your Pursuit hinges on knowing what you want. It is a forging ahead practice in which you have the power to decide the direction your life will take. The more open and honest you are, the faster you will achieve what you want.

> Your Pursuit hinges on knowing what you want. It is a forging ahead practice in which you have the power to decide the direction your life will take.

Ken's story highlights the importance of Your Pursuit:

I remember engaging a group of great people in some consulting work. The company was a professional service startup that worked diligently on business tools to create plans and resolve issues for its clients. Over multiple quarters, it became evident the team was creating misdirection, uncertainty, and indecisiveness for themselves. They had no idea where to take the company. It was like they were fishing without knowing the type of fish they wanted to catch or which equipment to use. With that being the case, they used whatever bait fit on the hook, taking in any and every type of customer. They weren't clear on the places to go to catch the right fish, instead putting in tons of effort to cast a wide marketing net and coming up empty-handed often. For them, fishing was an unplanned and meaningless endeavor. Navigating the fog and catching anything sizable was difficult without any formidable direction.

The same is true for any organization, from small to large or startup to legacy. The missing piece was a clear direction for the startup and their clients. Without knowing which direction to take, we were effectively going nowhere—and doing it fast while wasting precious resources. I was not their answer. They needed to be their answer. They needed to take time to explore what they really wanted. If they couldn't, their organization would not survive.

This lesson is cemented into my mind and guarantees that each one of my clients knows what direction they're heading for themselves and the organization. The louder and arguably more important lesson in this business example is that it holds true for individuals as well. Being directionless can kill. You must not only have a desire to pursue, but also know exactly what you are pursuing.

What Do You Want?

By now, you have a deep understanding of openness and honesty and how to create more of both in your life and relationships. You also understand how real communication is essential to doing better together. This is the time to pull everything together and make it actionable. But before we can make any of it work for you, there is one critical question you must answer: *What do you want?*

When you don't know what you want, you end up drifting directionlessly throughout life. And while that is certainly better than causing active harm, it leaves you powerless over your own destiny. You'll have given up the opportunity to design the life you want. Without knowing what you want, everyone else's influence on your life becomes so much greater than your own. The choice is to either run your life as you see fit or let everyone else do it for you and be left with little satisfaction in the end. To that end, Your Pursuit is the final practice of the Six Practices.

Think about your own life for a moment because, inevitably, that is where you maintain a high level of control. We know there is no controlling others—what they think, say, or do—so we must turn that attention inward. A lack of clarity around what you want will guarantee that you don't achieve and experience it. This is the quickest path to nowhere while exerting a tremendous amount of effort and believing you are headed somewhere. However, if going nowhere doesn't sound enjoyable to you, then you can leverage openness and honesty to accelerate your progress once you discover what you want.

Your Pursuit Is a Forging Ahead Practice

As your levels of openness and honesty rise using the other practices, you'll build up the momentum that propels you closer and closer to getting what you want. When we ask our clients, "What do you really want?" they respond with one of two answers:

> I don't know.
>
> *or*
>
> I want _____.

If we were to ask you those questions and you responded with "I don't know," you're in good company. There's a shocking number of people at varying stages of their lives who struggle to answer this question. It's okay to not have an immediate answer, but it's not okay to never have an answer when you want more out of life.

We simply cannot help each other or ourselves when we don't know what it is they or we want. No one can answer this question for you. No one can be you. This is about you. You might have some hard work to do exploring the answer through introspection and asking yourself difficult questions. No matter the case, please *enjoy* uncovering the answer. This is your opportunity to dream big and as far outside the box as you want.

If you want more clarity and certainty in your life, then you must take the time to explore the answer. Before you start using the Your Pursuit practice, set aside some quiet time to go deep. Use the Still you've already completed to help as a guide, or simply search your heart and soul for the answer. Similar to answering the Still, repeatedly ask yourself why until you get to the root of what you want. For example, if you want financial freedom, ask why. "So I don't feel shackled to my job." Why? "So I can have time for other passions." So on and so forth.

We encourage you to go a step further by splitting in half the circle that says "What do you really want?" and answering the question for both your work life and your personal life. We recommend you keep it to one answer for both work life and personal life. If you list fifty things, your effort toward each will be dismal, so keep it focused as best you can. The more focus you place on uncovering what you want, the higher the likelihood you will achieve it. Keep asking why until you discover the core reason behind what you want.

Here is a list of what clients have focused on, wanted, and achieved:

- I want to leave a legacy for my family.
- I desire better relationships.
- I'm seeking closeness with God.
- I want financial freedom.
- I want more time for myself.

Using the Your Pursuit model below, write down what you want in the circle to the right. If you don't know the exact answer now, put down your initial thoughts. The more you think about what it is you really want, the more opportunities will begin to form in your mind. Don't be afraid to dream big. It's amazing what happens when you write it down, so don't downplay your wants.

What do you really want?

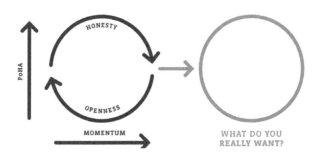

In the space below, write down what you need to be open and honest about to help you gain momentum toward your want. You may have to get creative, but most importantly, be open and honest.

Identify the next three steps you'll commit to, big or small:

Be Honest About:

1. _____
2. _____
3. _____

Be Open To:

1. _____
2. _____
3. _____

Let's look at this example of a client's Pursuit:

What do I really want? *A better job*
Why? *To make more money*
Why? *To have new experiences in my life*

Be Honest About:

1. The upward mobility at work
2. My current skills and gaps
3. A conversation with my boss and share with her

Become a CEO

WHAT DO YOU REALLY WANT?

Be Open To:

1. Taking criticism better and actively working on the feedback given
2. Positions at other organizations

3. Keeping my ears open for new challenges my company offers

You see, the more you know about what you want, the better you can plan the necessary steps to achieve it. It's like building a house. The more detailed the blueprint, the easier it is to execute the vision. No idea of what you want? No blueprint will be created. Imagine the type of mess you'd create by building a house without a proper blueprint. Then, why is it so common for us to build our lives without carefully planning out the foundational aspects of it?

With your answers written down, you've now become accountable to yourself. To take it to the next level, share Your Pursuit with the person in your life who will hold you accountable to these next steps. In your personal life, it may be a best friend, partner, or therapist. In your work life, it may be your boss, a coworker, a coach, or a close colleague.

Take action and get what you really want out of this life. Help others do the same for themselves. In doing so, we'll create a world in which dreams become reality. Enjoy thinking and building upon Your Pursuit.

You'll get closer and closer to your ideal reality as you become more honest with yourself about what you want. This will help you identify the true condition and make informed decisions. What you want is attainable, no matter how big you've dreamed, because you have deemed it a possibility. The more open you are to the ideas, feedback, and educational opportunities available to you, the more materials and tools you have at your disposal to achieve your wants.

In his book *Secrets of the Millionaire Mind*, T. Harv Eker offers a brilliant thought related to goals and commitments. He stresses the importance of dreaming big

> **What you want is attainable, no matter how big you've dreamed, because you have deemed it a possibility.**

but, more importantly, being 100 percent committed to it. Knowing what you want is great; now, you must ensure you are relentlessly committed to it.

Be aware that as you go, you keep evolving into new versions of you, possibly changing what you want. Keep close tabs on what your heart really wants, and use this practice as often as needed. We recommend reviewing and updating it every six months. You hold the power to design the life you want.

The Summit of Getting What You Want

Ken shares the following story:

In the early part of my career fixing and helping companies, I encountered one of the most important relationships of my life—my relationship with Bill Vander Velde. Bill was a co-owner of a company that had gotten stuck. It had been built from the ground up with a strong partnership and steady growth, but now was stagnant, and the partnership was struggling, to say the least.

I interviewed for a position at his company, Summit Landscape Management, and entered with nothing more than an "I can help" mentality. Upon interviewing, I remember seeing Bill haggard, tired, and worn out. He was in a tough spot and desperately needed someone's help in a way he never had before. He took a risk, shared his need for help, and hired me on a gamble. In a way, he became open to something, to someone else.

Upon joining his organization, and before anything else, we had to address the emotional toll of a failing partnership. Bill struggled to carry the weight of the organization while finding a way to engage his partner in solutions to save it. He waffled on saving the partnership and struggled to see how it could be salvaged. The two had grown distant and disengaged from one another. They were not willing to effectively communicate, which resulted in a downward spiral from a once beautiful partnership. It became clear to Bill that there were two very different visions for where Summit was going.

Looking at Bill, I asked him, "What do you really want?" He let out a big sigh and said, "I would like to run this company without my partner. I can do this in a way I think could be better for everyone."

Once Bill was clear on what he wanted, it was time to act. We held difficult and emotionally charged conversations to navigate through what the two really wanted. We got them in a room together and had them lean into more honesty about the issue than they ever had before. As it turned out, his partner shared a similar want. He was ready to step away from the business. Once the true condition was on the table, we created and executed plans for a buyout. After so much pain and mistrust, difficult negotiations, and a few coarse words, the two experienced what it was like to move toward what they really wanted.

By embracing honesty, Bill expressed what he wanted. His ex-partner did the same. Collectively, they achieved a desired outcome. Embracing openness, Bill accepted outside help and listened without reservation. He no longer carried the weight of all ideas and decisions. He surrounded himself with a team ready to help Summit move forward.

After solving this problem, we began to poke at the issue of profit. Bill hadn't opened his books to an internal person other than his now ex-partner in seventeen years. We diagnosed the issues and sat in the true condition of poor decision-making and lack of oversight. We examined the market and realized how far off pricing was from our competitors. We were doing business and losing money, so we adjusted the pricing to have a favorable margin.

Amidst all this focus on fixing profit, Bill was determined to keep all his staff. He ate the losses believing that the people around him would help row toward the company goals. He formed a leadership team that cared about the success of the business and began to experience having others helping him get what he wanted. He moved into a less guarded, more transparent, open and honest relationship with his staff. All this change and focus created survival for Summit. It also created additional wages for employees and more jobs for the community.

The leadership team had open and honest conversations about quoting, billing, and sales-related issues. Because of the team's willingness to accept criticism and investigate other ways to succeed, we gained more financial advantages. As the financial picture and culture improved, so did Bill's stress. He became happier, had more fun, and was able to give more time to his family and friends. He was starting to get everything he wanted. But there was one last puzzle piece: the future of Summit.

A couple of years later, I again asked Bill, "Hey Bill, what do you really want?" Bill had evolved into a new version of himself, and so, naturally, the answer had changed. He wanted the company to be secure, with great employees and hoped that his son would take an interest. So, we got to work.

To this day, I smile at his success and at those around him who benefited from it. In our most recent session, we reflected on the success of the past year.

Bill responded with, "What more can I ask for than to come to work and do it with my son every day?" The heaviness and stress from before have vanished from his face. He looks younger than when I met him ten years ago.

Bill and his team are still on their Pursuit, answering new questions around what they want, embracing more openness and more honesty, and designing a better life for themselves and others. We are honored to be a part of the journey to help them achieve their hearts' desires. We want that for you and for every single person in your life too. Use the Pursuit to get there, and enlist those around you. Watch as your life transforms, and know that you made it happen.

Our challenge to you:
Use Your Pursuit to get crystal clear on
what you really want.
Check-in every six months to ensure
you're moving in the right direction.

PART III

Openness and Honesty in Action

12

Versions of You: *Change Is Inevitable*

C hange is an inevitable and natural part of our lives. Always. Every single minute of every single day. Whether you are aware of it or not, your subconscious, like a computer operating system, is always running in the background and firing on all cylinders. The current version of you, the one reading this book and absorbing the words on this page, will shortly become the newest version of you, leading the way to yet another future iteration of you. While reading this chapter, and even this paragraph, it is likely you'll learn something new that could change your mind or reinforce ideas you already believe.

Either way, change occurs in these moments. Some of you may recognize this as positive, while some of you may see it as negative. Regardless of your perspective, you cannot argue with the fact that change is an inevitable constant. However, it is just as inevitable that you have a choice to make in this process. This crucial decision empowers you to wake up every day and own your life—you can be the victim of change or the champion of it.

It is because of this fact that we know that changing how the world communicates is possible. We've seen it happen with hundreds of our clients and in our closest relationships. With enough people educated in openness and honesty and equipped with the Six

You can be the victim of change or the champion of it.

Practices, we know that real communication is accessible to all. We have an opportunity to pivot together as a society and do away with Fake You and the Wall.

Let's first look at how we've individually reached this point in our lives.

As you investigate your own past, you'll recognize many versions of yourself. That doesn't mean you were someone else; you were still you throughout each iteration of your life. But you certainly lived as a different version of yourself, with unique perspectives based on your experiences at that given moment. You have been evolving through every moment of your life. Many changes are taking place that individually create one new version of you. Many times, you're upgrading to a bigger, better version, and other times to a more corrupt, self-deprecating one.

The beauty of this is that you can largely dictate your changes. You can impact who you will become tomorrow and ten years from now. The facets of change are far and wide, from where you live to how you speak, from physical appearance to social circles, from growth to decay. The simple blessing of waking up this morning creates new opportunities. The you of yesterday had not seen today's sunlight or breathed today's air.

Even the most stubborn "I'm not willing to change" types experience daily changes. Some are not as visible, like the decay of a body over years or muscle development through intentional training. These changes do not happen all at once but rather occur in the same manner we build the foundation for a home—one brick at a time. Eventually, though, we lay enough bricks that our growth becomes visible. Every repeated conversation, piece of acquired knowledge, or hobby helps you evolve. Think about it this way: You may move from version 2.35 to 2.36 after perfecting a golf swing or from version 1.95 to version 2.25 upon reading a new book. No matter the jump, big or small, the evolution is continual.

Every moment of your life led you to this point. In large, you shaped each of those iterations through your decisions. You made choices and became the byproduct of your choices and the choices of others. Going forward, know that you have the power to influence all the future iterations of you. For many of you, realizing this will awaken your mind to the real possibility and influence you have to create the life you truly want.

The Science Behind It

From a scientific perspective, neuroplasticity reinforces this change. Neuroplasticity, as defined by the National Library of Medicine, "refers to the brain's ability to modify, change, and adapt both structure and function throughout life and in response to experience."[1] This occurs through the neural pathways in our brain, which are unique to every person on this planet. As we create and repeat the habits and systems in our lives, the neural pathways that correlate with those actions develop deeper grooves that make it easier to repeat them. Muscle memory is a great example of neuroplasticity.

At first, a certain set of movements feels foreign to our bodies. It takes concentrated effort and thought to complete them. As we repeat them, these isolated sets of movements eventually become one smooth motion. This can be helpful to create efficiencies, such as our morning routines and our drives to work. But they become dangerous when we settle into them as a way of life.

This is why it's important to pay close attention to ourselves as we experience changes and evolutions. Should we move down a negative path, it will only become easier and easier for our brains to run down that neural pathway. This is also why it can be hard, at first, to rid ourselves of Fake You and eliminate the Wall because some of those pathways already run deep in our brains. The brain is an incredibly efficient organ, doing its best to run on autopilot as often as possible to conserve energy. This method was a great help to our ancestors, ensuring they had enough energy to outthink a predator when necessary. However, in our modern lives, we need to consider how much this wiring helps as well as hurts us. We must understand the power we have at any time to choose a different direction and create a new neural pathway. This opportunity is always available to us.

We do not stop changing once we reach adulthood. So long as we are alive, even in our later years, our brains remain a place of change and innovation. We have the choice to strengthen certain neural pathways and create new ones. Each new version of ourselves creates a deeper groove and is a vote for who we're aiming to become. So long as we live, we can shape the way in which our brain works and how we grow.

And as for the other part of neuroplasticity's definition, *in response to experience*, what we must recognize is the *in response* part. We can decide our response to the experiences we have each day. That decision will influence the ways in which our brain changes.

Ken shares the following story from his youth:

When I was sixteen years old, I dreamed of being the CEO of Pepsi-Cola. After all, I loved their soda and their advertisements. I was at an impressionable age. There was no real basis for what CEO even meant to me, nor was I taking my current status in life to reach that goal seriously. However, having this knowledge about myself propelled me to take an interest in business. I began taking small steps toward fulfilling that dream. At that young age, I purchased business magazines and read up on the latest trends. This created new neural pathways in my brain. I'd chosen learning with a slant toward business. These activities added to a slightly more evolved version of me. Let's call that version 1.45, and I continued building upon that evolution.

By seventeen, I took a management position at a pizza shop and forced myself into responsibility. It was one of the first times I took a significant risk to push myself to evolve. I willingly put myself in an uncomfortable challenge. My brain had to adapt. This tactic has proven extremely useful throughout my entire life. At that time, I didn't really know what the hell I was doing. I wasn't thinking about becoming a high-level leader, nor how I could think deeper about other people. But I did know I had to gain some experience in management to grow. These weren't major leaps or bounds forward but rather slight adjustments in making progress on my desires.

Years later, I found myself with a degree in business and wanting to be in a more executive-level position. However, I wasn't taking any meaningful steps toward that end result. While earning the degree, I had taken a job bartending. It provided some great short-term financial benefits but didn't really help my long-term vision. In fact, my long-term vision had taken a back seat.

I was enjoying the minimal responsibility, the drinking, the partying, and all the convenience advertised from that lifestyle. It was an easy habit to perpetuate. Much of it led to emptiness and, looking back, purposelessness. I was killing my mind and body with many of the choices I had made unconsciously. I was hurting my chances of becoming who I had dreamed of. I recall serving drinks when a waitress, Kristina, stopped me for a second and said, "I'm surprised you're still a bartender. I really pictured you in a business role, leading a company or something."

That was my wake-up call. What she likely thought was a fleeting comment sent a shockwave through my system. That unforgettable moment was the instant a new neural pathway was created. My aspirations were clearly not aligned with my current state. At the present, bartending was my trajectory. If I had let it, my brain would have ridden that career choice for the rest of my life. It was nowhere near the trajectory of becoming a Pepsi-Cola CEO. Kristina's comment snapped me out of my directionless haze and into my true condition. It was evident I wanted something different and more for my life but was making zero effort in evolving that dream. I felt called to something different, more natural to who I truly was within. But, I was finding myself stuck in a comfortable pattern of pouring drinks and socializing late into the night. Version 3.15 of Ken decided to get moving. I needed my next evolution.

Jobs were scarce at the time for someone with my limited experience. Nothing seemed to match my desire. So, I continued my education. At the very least, I could progress and evolve through learning more. I pushed my brain to put its neuroplasticity to work. While gaining a higher education, I began to search out professional experiences, accepting an assistantship at a trade center and a management role for a rent-a-car company. All the while, I continued slinging drinks for the extra income, now knowing it served only that purpose.

Each of those experiences offered growth, and each evolution of myself led me closer and closer to what I had only previously dreamed about. Higher education gave me a well-rounded viewpoint on a variety of topics in the business industry. I had experiences with fellow students and felt compelled to grow, learn, and collaborate with them. Version 3.23 of Ken emerged. The assistantship gave me real-life experience with clients and world exporting knowledge. Version 3.28. The management role at the rent-a-car company was a whole new industry, with an entirely different management approach that enhanced my sales ability, my stress management, and customer service. Version 3.35.

Fast forward through several more versions, creating a countless set of new neural pathways, and five hundred-plus stories later, I arrive at the present-day Ken. I am not a Pepsi-Cola CEO, and in hindsight, that's great. Professionally, I've ended up helping hundreds of leaders so far. Personally, I have a family of four and live a blessed life. By all standard measures, and more importantly to me, I've "made it." This isn't to brag or boast but rather to illustrate that the choice is yours. You can build upon where you are right now and set yourself on the course you desire. It does not matter whether you have strayed from the path you once dreamed of or a completely new one has appeared. Where I've landed is better than I had dreamed, and I want that for you.

My reason for sharing this is to encourage you to be open and honest. Honest with where you are and where you want to go. Open to the experiences and opportunities life is presenting to you. Embracing openness and honesty will better help you form the change you really desire. You can impose change and begin to carve the kind of future you want.

All the experiences I've had and my responses to them have led me to this current version of Ken, one who is clear on how to influence my future and enjoy the success in where I have ended up. Each of your previous evolutions has compounded to where you are today. Whether you view the past in a positive light or not, it was what propelled you to this point. You are who you are today because of your past experiences and how each one of those has shaped who you are now.

Openness and Honesty's Impact on Growth

When you remain honest, living life as truly and freely yourself, you are better informing yourself for the changes and experiences to come. The opposite holds true as well. If we move through life being Fake You, we are actively moving further away from the person we want to be. We begin to disengage from and lose access to our true condition. And the farther we move from that, the more difficult it becomes to return to being truly and freely ourselves. Even the slightest trajectory off from honesty can send our lives down paths we never desired.

Don't underestimate the power you have to direct your life, from compounding micro-moments to monumental shifts. The more you know yourself, the true condition, and act in the space of being truly and freely yourself, the easier it is to navigate the future. You're building yourself rooted in honesty, and that is a stronger foundation than any façade can provide.

You can and will keep working and focusing on you, but you're not in a vacuum. Let's not forget our shared world as we continually change. When you are around others who want to grow and evolve, you can expect yourself to follow suit. Your mind becomes a sponge to all that circulates in it, especially when you've developed a strong ability to knock down

> **Don't underestimate the power you have to direct your life, from compounding micro-moments to monumental shifts.**

the Wall. You'll begin to notice the transformational ideas around you.

Opportunities have always been there, but with openness, you're finally able to discover them. You begin filling your life with growth-minded conversations when those around you hold similar values. You will more frequently challenge your status quo. You will be expedited to the next positive version of yourself nearly every time you engage with someone else who also desires a more positive outcome for their life. You will constantly be reaching a higher state of mind when you are surrounded by others doing the same.

The same holds true if you spend time with those who regularly choose decay, negativity, or stagnation. Your mind is at risk of being filled with growth-stunting opposition or, worse, regression. Who you wanted to become can slip away as you accept or frequently return to these poor relationships.

You will constantly operate in a lower state of mind. Consider who in your life challenges you and those who have resigned themselves to the status quo. Which group helps evolve you and which deepens the neural pathways that have gotten you stuck? Again, it comes back to the future version of you being highly correlated to the decisions you make today. The choice is yours; blame no one else.

Thus far, we have only discussed ourselves in terms of neuroplasticity, change, and evolutions—how only you are impacted through your own actions. But if we are continuously changing and evolving ourselves, then the same holds true for every other person with whom we share this world. Eight billion people on this planet are progressing and evolving into their own next versions. Because we evolve and create new neural pathways in response to every experience in our existence, we must consider the high level of impact we have on others, most especially those closest to us.

When we live with openness and honesty, we know we're doing our best to be a net positive contributor to our world and to those around us. The opposite is true as well. When we show up to spaces as Fake You, we dilute the experience for everyone and negatively affect everyone. We create a lack of clarity for other people. The trickle-down effect is monumental. By acting from a place of insincerity and deceit, we screw up their access to the true condition for the sake of ourselves. It is critical to own what we are bringing to the table and to the world at large.

As we increase our ability to be open, we create spaces where individuals can exist as they are. However, if we constantly impose our will, our honesty, and ourselves on others, we leave little space for them. When the Wall rises, we no longer exchange with them meaningfully and can't help them because we are no longer

When we live with openness and honesty, we know we're doing our best to be a net positive contributor to our world and to those around us.

putting our needs and wants on pause for them. When two people come together in conversation, there are two separate participants. Because of that, there will be disagreements and differences. We can treat it as an opportunity to understand someone else. We can take the time to appreciate another person and their experiences. Differences and conflict aren't inherently negative. It is an opportunity to learn and grow together.

If you choose to be 100 percent honest and 100 percent closed-minded, you can expect to remain stagnant. If there is only space for your thoughts and opinions, then there is no space for the other person to recognize and be open to what you have to say. They cannot be in the same space with you because you've hogged it all. However, when you allow them to also have their thoughts and opinions, mutual respect will exist, and you'll no longer find yourself alone. If you can understand their viewpoint, then your understanding of the world grows.

Allowing others to share space and bring themselves to the table is critical. Just as we have new experiences, responses to those experiences, and create new versions of ourselves, so too does everyone else. This means that each time we encounter someone, even a person we've known our entire life, they will be a unique version of themselves we have not yet met. The change may only be a slight contrast, but it is a change all the same. When we allow them to live out the changes within themselves and their lives, we can engage in ways that foster a more productive and meaningful interaction. Both people, allowed to be heard and respected, will grow together no matter how short or long the relationship is.

To that end, how will you choose to use your experiences and ability to change? Whatever you choose will be how you evolve, and much of your future depends on what you consume. Our minds are constantly consuming, endlessly, even as we sleep. Our bodies are changing and adapting too. And the same goes for our souls. Put simply, if your mind, body, and soul are constantly consuming, then what are you choosing to consume?

Is it negative or positive?
Are you choosing gluttony or nutrition?
Is your spiritual cup full or empty?

As you are building the next version of you, think about what you are using as building blocks. The very foundation of yourself is being built with what you consume.

Evolving in an Intentional Way

Thankfully, we have a choice in what our minds invite and accept into our lives. Once we process the experience or information, we then have a second choice—what do we do with it?

We can take that experience and turn it into a net positive. We can perpetuate positive thoughts or negative thoughts about any exchange. To the degree which we choose positive outcomes directly correlates to how our thinking grows in a positive direction. On the flip side, to the degree we consume negative outcomes, our thinking will grow in a negative direction. It is all compounding. And it is all well within our realm of control. Are your experiences happening *to you* or *for you*?

Here and moving forward, as we choose to grow and evolve, we'll need to equip ourselves with openness and honesty and pair them with a commitment and desire for more. To better ensure we reach the future we desire, we must strengthen these two aspects in our life. Understanding the impact that our experiences and choices have on us and the power to choose our response, to be open and honest.

13

Becoming Masterful Communicators:
Applying the Six Practices

Every way of life involves interaction between human beings. There are spoken and unspoken rules. Up until this point, as a society, we've put little thought into how we communicate and whether it's working. We are committed to changing this and hope you are too. Through what you've learned in our time together and now being equipped with the Six Practices, you have the choice to be intentional and become a masterful communicator.

Across the board, there are examples of people who share this world with you who have made real commitments to create more open and honest environments, eliminate the divide, create real communication, and experience real relationships.

- SJA Solutions leadership team went all-in on communication. They constantly push themselves to understand each other better and experience a smoother flow of communication. Since 2020, they've created year-over-year financial growth. But perhaps more importantly, even through their most troubling times, the team has experienced positive impacts on their mental health because they're committed to always being open and honest with each other.

- Ken and Ilse continue to have incredible disagreements, but their marriage will stand the tests of time because of their commitment to communicate with one another. They will say what needs to be said and hear what the other one is saying.

- During an exit interview at Deksia, a soon-to-be former employee thanked the team. She was grateful for all she had learned and the valuable lessons she'd carry with her because of Deksia and its people. The team takes great pride in all the staff they retain and all those who leave, knowing they've made a positive impact on their lives. They're acutely aware that their culture doesn't just remain within their office walls but reaches areas all over the world.

- By remaining open, Father Joshua experiences more of the world and connects deeply with those who might never have engaged in conversation with him. Because of this, he's able to share the love he feels from God with those who may never step inside his church nor have ever known what it's like to have someone willing to hear them simply for who they are. He is casting aside the divisiveness and creating more belonging in the world.

- Summit Landscape experiences a record number of returning staff who realize that their culture is willing to grow, learn, and deepen real communication, unlike any other place they may have left for. Those who left came to see that the grass really wasn't greener and returned even more committed to giving their all at work. Summit is willing to take them back, exhibiting an understanding of the human condition that many organizations do not.

- Grace and Eric, still in the first stages of marriage, are creating the strongest foundation for the years and trials to come. Although they often find themselves on opposing sides of ideology, they continue to engage in the conversation. They're clear that because of the commitment they've made, together they will side against a problem, never against each other. Their ability to create real communication means they can both remain connected and maintain different opinions.

These are just a few examples among millions where the pursuit of openness and honesty is changing how the world communicates. Each of these brief snapshots has a common thread: They all have people at the helm committed to real communication. We discussed choice earlier with respect to our growth, constant evolution, and Your Pursuit. Your choice to embrace real communication alone is a step forward that will positively impact each community, organization, and relationship you're in. You can intentionally shape any space you occupy. We all can embrace and encourage more open and honest environments, rich with real communication.

Living in an open and honest way allows everything you take in to be a positive building block within your life. As you become more truly and freely yourself, happiness has a greater chance to take root. As you listen without reservation, you eliminate the need to control the unpredictable parts of life, and every conversation becomes easier. Life's challenges arrive with more clarity and are easier to overcome.

One conversation filled with real communication gives you a taste of the freedom two people can experience. One open and honest relationship at a time transforms and strengthens a small community. One organization embracing real communication impacts hundreds to thousands of employees, customers, stakeholders, and so on. The more the skills of openness, honesty, and real communication take root in our society, the more freedom we will create for ourselves and those around us.

As a whole, we will do better together. Because people everywhere are more heard and respected, lives everywhere are granted a whole new level of freedom that this world has yet to experience. Instead of squashing and inhibiting the flow of communication, we are setting it free.

If you are at the helm of an organization, this is your responsibility to all the people in your care. This is what it means to be a leader. You have a choice to stop serving the ego that blinds you to the rest of the people surrounding you. So many leaders are hung up on their own achievements and desire for power that they trounce the very lives that encircle them. A lonely seat at the top is as much a choice as it is to embrace and enjoy the humans within your care.

If you are at the helm of the household, you are tasked with creating strength in your home through real communication. You know how easily impressionable our minds are and the impact we have on others. One little challenge can throw our foundation off in an instant. As you navigate differing opinions and disagreements, young minds will be watching. They will see if two people choose to disconnect and avoid the regular challenges of life or if those two people stay in it and fight for understanding and resolve. True strength is found in the latter.

A lonely seat at the top is as much a choice as it is to embrace and enjoy the humans within your care.

If you lead or impact anyone else's life, real communication is one of the most important gifts you can share with that person. Agreeing to be open and honest, using the Agreement, is equivalent to giving someone the complete right to be themselves. You have cleared a path to help someone else and given them the space to be more comfortable in their own skin and more confident in their right to share their views. If you believe that being 100 percent truly and freely yourself is one of life's greatest accomplishments, then be a contributing member to someone else's greatest accomplishment.

Given the monumental responsibility of creating real communication, you must be aware that it takes effort and repeated practice. If you keep it simple, the task is far less daunting. Remember, you are after both parties being 100 percent open and 100 percent honest. By keeping it to just these two components, it is much clearer when a conversation derails out of openness and honesty. The goal is to continuously create more moments of real communication. By doing so, you are making the intentional choice to shape the relationship rather than allow it to devolve into the worst of our human instincts.

We all stand to gain when our foundation is one built on openness and honesty, where the uniqueness of all the cultures across our world shines. Where we experience peace because someone else's way of life is no longer a threat to our own. We stand grounded in ourselves and connected to each person who does the same.

The conversations you'll have moving forward will become easier and freer flowing—including the most difficult ones. Each person trusts that what is being said is honest and received with openness. You'll see fewer issues being swept under the rug, more voices being heard and respected, and more access to the true condition.

When we know what the other person says is honest, we do not doubt or second-guess. We no longer need to revisit a conversation in our minds over and over to dissect if that is what the person really meant or if we missed a hidden message. This makes it easier for everyone to move on to the next version of themselves and elevate the collective as a result. As it's commonly said, "A rising tide lifts all boats." When we create the next evolution of ourselves in a positive trajectory, we do the same for all those we encounter and push our society further into one where everyone can do the same.

By now, you've heard plenty of stories about how teams, organizations, and relationships lacked openness and honesty and shifted to embracing real communication. With the Six Practices, we've made real communication and real relationships accessible to you. We've made tangible what was previously ambiguous and unnecessarily difficult. These Practices will equip you in Your Pursuit of Honesty. We've shared them all throughout this book, but here they are all together for easy reference as you revisit this repeatedly:

The Agreement (Chapter 6)

- Forging Ahead Practice
- The Agreement is a simple, powerful script to follow at the outset of any conversation to achieve real communication.
- When: Use as often as needed. It ought to be a regular part of your life.

The Assessment (Chapter 7)

- Reflective Practice
- The Assessment is the measurable approach to openness and honesty. It will uncover your ability to deliver and receive real communication.
- When: Complete every six months

Fake You (Chapter 8)

- In the Moment Practice
- Fake You is the façade we project rather than being 100 percent honest.
- When: After the initial reflection, rid yourself of Fake You every moment you recognize it showing up.

The Wall (Chapter 9)

- In the Moment Practice
- The Wall is the divide we create between ourselves and others rather than being 100 percent open.
- When: After the initial reflection, eliminate the Wall every moment you recognize it showing up.

The Still (Chapter 10)

- Reflective Practice
- The Still helps you think, be present, and access the true condition.
- When: Complete every six months

Your Pursuit (Chapter 11)

- Forging Ahead Practice
- Your Pursuit hinges on knowing what you want. The more open and honest you are, the faster you achieve what you want.
- When: Complete every six months

You now have the practices, the education, and the stories as proof that this is how we will eliminate the divide between ourselves and everyone else. It is our responsibility, every one of us, to create a more open and honest world. As Your Pursuit unfolds, you are tasked with being the example of why a life rooted in openness and honesty is what's best for this world. Know that we are by your side, along with countless others, doing the exact same every day that we are gifted.

You are a part of a movement that is changing how the world communicates. This is how we will do better together.

Now that you have this knowledge, what will you do next?

Endnotes

1. Brene Brown, *Daring Greatly: How the Courage to Be Vulnerable Transforms the Way We Live, Love, Parent, and Lead* (Avery, 2015).

2. "The Loneliness Epidemic Persists: A Post-Pandemic Look at the State of Loneliness Among U.S. Adults," Cigna, accessed May 5, 2024, https://newsroom.thecignagroup.com/loneliness-epidemic-persists-post-pandemic-look.

3. "Our Epidemic of Loneliness and Isolation 2023," US Surgeon General's Advisory on the Healing Effects of Social Connection and Community, accessed May 12, 2024, https://www.hhs.gov/sites/default/files/surgeon-general-social-connection-advisory.pdf.

   Graph is borrowed from Kannan, Viji Diane and Peter J. Veazie, "US trends in social isolation, social engagement, and companionship – nationally and by age, sex, race/ethnicity, family income, and work hours, 2003–2020," SSM - Population Health, Volume 21, 2023, https://doi.org/10.1016/j.ssmph.2022.101331.

4. Evan W. Carr et al., "The Value of Belonging at Work," *Harvard Business Review*, December 16, 2019, https://hbr.org/2019/12/the-value-of-belonging-at-work.

5. Compiled from Assessment data by Know Honesty. © 2024 Know Honesty.

Acknowledgments

Ken's Thank Yous

To my Maker, knowing that my very existence is too improbable to be coincidence puts me in constant awe of Your glory. Thank You for smiling on us, even though we never deserve it.

Ilse, I thank God for you, your courage, and your ability to love, even in the toughest of times. You and me, no matter what!

Mila and Dax, be sure to love, dream, be honest, and thankful in all you do. I love you like crazy.

To my stoic German, Lutheran, retired engineer, former military, and loving father, thank you for the boundless sacrifices you've made for me. I love you!

To my clients, thanks for having faith in me and being part of our open and honest journey. Each one of you has played a role in what Know Honesty has become. I'm grateful for you. You know the drill: email, call, or text anytime.

To our vendors and partners, you've gotten us here! Thanks for embracing The Agreement. You've made us stronger than we could have ever imagined by constantly challenging us and sharing your honesty.

To Grace, from caring for my kiddos to being my business partner, it's been an incredible journey. And it's only just begun...

Grace's Thank Yous

Eric, thank you for standing by my side through this journey. You've never wavered in your belief of me and I couldn't do it without you. Te amo!

Mom, thank you for teaching me how to care for others and stepping into new conversations with me. Love you forever.

Dad, I wish you were here to see this. Thank you for guiding me from the beyond. Keep stopping by to say hi. I love you.

My family, without whom I am nothing. I know I don't say it enough, but thank you for all that you do. I love you all.

Sam and Liv, y'all are day ones. I love you both.

To my clients, thank you for welcoming me into your team. It's a privilege to serve you, and I'm grateful every day.

To all our partners, vendors, and champions, thank you for making us into what we are today. We couldn't do it without you.

Ken, you've bet on me so many times a million thank yous wouldn't be enough. You're a life changer, and I'm honored to work alongside you.

And finally, thank you to YOU for reading this book. You've entered a new world of connection, and we'll be encouraging you at every step.

About the Authors

Ken Bogard founded Know Honesty® and owns a success-ful EOS® Franchise, both essential pieces for changing how our world communicates. For over 25 years, his enthusiasm for results, extensive experience, and entrepreneurial grit have provided the momentum for organizations, business owners, and employees to achieve what they want out of life.

Ken's Know Honesty approach enhances the lives of hun-dreds of professionals, delivers significant financial gains for companies, improves leadership collaboration, and is creating a movement. He currently lives in Michigan with his incred-ible wife, Ilse, and their two children, Mila and Dax.

Connect with Ken at KnowHonesty.com.

Grace Gavin is co-founder of Know Honesty® and guides people toward becoming masterful communicators every day. From her humble roots growing up on a dairy farm to now working with all levels of leadership, she has a special ability to ask the right questions to help audiences go deeper and uncover what's blocking them from creating real communication.

Grace also serves on several boards and enjoys volunteering. In her spare time, she can be found devouring books, gardening, and spending time with family and friends. She lives in Michigan with her husband, Eric, and their dog, Nova.

Connect with Grace at KnowHonesty.com.

DO YOU KNOW YOUR NUMBERS?

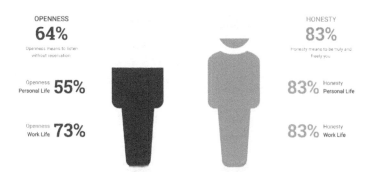

OPENNESS
64%
Openness means to listen
without reservation

Openness
Personal Life **55%**

Openness
Work Life **73%**

HONESTY
83%
Honesty means to be truly and
freely you

83% Honesty
Personal Life

83% Honesty
Work Life

By taking the Pursuit of Honesty® Assessment, you'll get your:

+ Real time data
+ Fake You and The Wall ratios
+ Work and personal percentages
+ Personalized Open and Honest Model

To take The Assessment or update your scores, please visit knowhonesty.com/assessment or scan the QR code.

Create a Culture of Real Communication

Are you ready to experience openness and honesty in real time?

Ken and Grace, the Open and Honest Experts, are available for select offerings, including:

+ Keynotes   + Author Talks
+ Workshops   + Breakouts
+ Seminars   + Custom Engagements

And join them for the exclusive
Become a Masterful Communicator Workshop
an immersively one day event to change
how you communicate.

**FIND THE
NEXT EVENT
NEAR YOU
TODAY!**

OPEN AND HONEST
UNBOUND
NEWSLETTER

Your monthly dose
of real communication

SUBSCRIBE NOW

Be the first to receive:
+ Thought pieces
+ Timely videos
+ Inspiring quotes
+ Know Honesty updates
+ and so much more!

Let's Get Social

Today's platforms are designed to be divisive,
but Ken and Grace are changing the conversation.

Connect with them on:

@KenBogard @GraceGavin
@KnowHonesty

KnowHonesty.com

THIS BOOK IS PROTECTED INTELLECTUAL PROPERTY

The author of this book values Intellectual Property. The book you just read is protected by Easy IP®, a proprietary process, which integrates blockchain technology giving Intellectual Property "Global Protection." By creating a "Time-Stamped" smart contract that can never be tampered with or changed, we establish "First Use" that tracks back to the author.

Easy IP® functions much like a Pre-Patent™ since it provides an immutable "First Use" of the Intellectual Property. This is achieved through our proprietary process of leveraging blockchain technology and smart contracts. As a result, proving "First Use" is simple through a global and verifiable smart contract. By protecting intellectual property with blockchain technology and smart contracts, we establish a "First to File" event.

Protected By Easy IP®

LEARN MORE AT EASYIP.TODAY

Made in United States
Cleveland, OH
30 January 2025

13876390R00128